Little Buttons Telling Big Stories

By Catherine Pincott-Allen

A Field Detectives' Investigation 2025

First published in Great Britain in 2025

© The Field Detectives 2025

Lost Voices Publishing

The authors assert the moral right to be identified as the authors of this work

ISBN 978-1-7385568-5-4

Typeset using, Arial, Arial Rounded, Bell, Bodoni, Bookman Old Style, Calibri, Century Schoolbook, Comic Sans, Elephant, Engravers, Franklin Gothic, Gabriola, Gills Sans, Georgia, Liverpool, Lucida Calligraphy, Old English Text, Opti Romana, Playbill, Rockwell, Scotch Roman, Type Keys

Images are public domain or author's own photographs

Front cover copyright © The Field Detectives

No part of this publication may be reproduced, stored in a retrieval system, or transmitted in any form or by any means, electronic, mechanical, photocopying, recording or otherwise, without the authors' prior permission.

All rights reserved

www.the-field-detectives.com

Contents

Introduction

Nottingham Tailors

Alexander – Nottingham	9 – 11
A Barnfield – Nottingham	12 – 13
F W Beet & Co – Market St – Nottingham	14 – 16
James Bell – Nottingham	17 – 18
P Benjamin – 24 Hockley	19 – 21
Thomas Bird – Nottingham	22 – 24
Carey & Nephew – Nottingham	25 – 30
Carey Parker – Nottingham	
Carey Parker & Tirbutt – Nottingham	
A G Carrington – Nottingham	31 – 33
Dixon & Parker	34 – 39
T Finn & Son – Nottingham	40 – 42
W Gabbatiss – Nottingham	43 – 44
R Goldman – Nottingham	45 – 48
W P Groves – Nottingham	49 – 51
Kirk & Son – Nottingham	52 – 54
Liverseege – Nottingham	55 – 56
Manderfield – Nottingham	57 – 61
Matthews & Co – Nottingham	62 – 63
S & J Monk – Nottingham	64 – 67
Noddall – Newark	68 – 71
Porter & Co – Nottingham	72 – 74
T Sharp – Nottingham	75 – 76
W W Sibley – Nottingham	77 – 80
W Sibley Junr. – Nottingham	
Wilson & Son – Nottingham	81 – 83
W G Wilson – Nottingham	
Wilson – Angel Row	

Tailors From Other Towns

Atkinson & Son – Durham	85 – 86
George Binns – Sheffield	87 – 90
George Brown – Barnsley	91 – 93
Cooper – Glossop	94 – 97
R S Gold – Warwick	98 – 100
J Hawkridge – Derby	101 – 102
Headland & Co – Derby	103 – 105
Hill Bros – Old Bond Street	106 – 109
Humphreys & Crook – Haymarket	110 – 113
J W Lidgett – Wainfleet	114 – 116
Meyer & Mortimer – London & Edinburgh	117 – 120
H Poole & Co – Savill Row	121 – 122
J G Rowan – Greenock	123 – 124
Salanson – Conduit Street	125 – 126
Tautz & Son – Oxford Street	127 – 130
J & W Todd – Bourne	131 – 133
J Willson – Horncastle	134 – 137

A Haberdasher & A Pawnbroker

R James•Dealer – Hockley	139
T Wood – Chapel Bar	140 – 141
Stitches in Time	142
Acknowledgements	143
1901 Map of Nottingham	144 – 145
Also by the Author	146

INTRODUCTION

The Field Detectives have been surveying the fields around South Nottinghamshire since 1999. Over the years, one of the themes that emerged from our historic landscape investigations is that every field tells a story. Our portfolio of field survey reports details many of those stories and some of the fascinating mysteries we have discovered along the way. Metal detecting and field walking are pursuits that take you into the realms of time travel. One field might have something to say about the Roman occupation, another perhaps suggests a medieval story, and a neighbouring one might offer an opportunity to learn more about life in Britain during the Victorian era. Every field most certainly has a story to tell, and the artefacts from these fields, if examined carefully enough, can tell us something about the people who might have used them.

One such artefact is a small four-holed button. These inconspicuous objects, which are often heavily encrusted and difficult to decipher, tend not to attract attention as they do not gleam and sparkle. I suspect that many of them are regularly discarded as rubbish and confined to the refuse bin, but as this book shows, they are worthy of special attention because they do have some amazing stories to tell about the people who were associated with them. When we first started to compile this book, we began from the premise that the little buttons in question, measuring 12-15 mm in diameter, were tailors' buttons made to order by the 19th-century button-making firms operating out of London and Birmingham. This initial hypothesis was informed by the findings featured in button research publications, metal detecting and mudlark websites, related social media forums, and a fabulous online resource in Australia. By all accounts, these little buttons were being universally described as tailor's trousers/braces buttons. From the 1840s onwards, button manufacturers began to create branded buttons for tailors, often featuring the tailor's name and place of business. It was a practice that eventually evolved into a tradition, especially for those who sought to promote their business as a bespoke tailoring service. The buttons became a vehicle for advertising a tailor's designer clothing and for letting customers know where their high-quality garments were made.

Without jumping the gun towards adopting a preformed conclusion, we decided to focus on each of the buttons from our landscape study collection in turn, so we could then interrogate the names and places that had been branded on them as a family history research investigation. We wanted to know if they were all tailors' buttons, as we had initially been led to believe, and to see if they could tell us something about the people who were associated with them. If we could narrow down the timeline regarding their production and identify the firms that made them, then that would be an additional bonus.

With a name and place to start from, the journey of discovery did at least offer an avenue to pursue. This book tells the stories that emerged through many months of research, and thanks to those little buttons, people came back to life, most of whom were long forgotten. The first story to tell is how those little buttons found their way onto the fields in South Nottinghamshire in the first place.

The Grantham Canal

In the spring of 1797, following years of construction that presented huge social, engineering and financial challenges, the Grantham Canal was officially opened for business. This navigable link between the towns of Grantham and Nottingham promised cheaper coal supplies to the region, along with cheap imports of lime. In addition, there was an agricultural bonus in the form of cargoes of night soil from the overflowing privies of Nottingham for use as fertiliser on the fields.

A stark reference to the tough life that the canal cutters (those who dug out the canals by hand) had to endure reads, *'The daily pay for a cutter was around two shillings; for this he would be expected to move upwards of fourteen tonnes of soil.'* I don't know about you, but after a day in the garden, I'm ready for a cup of tea!

By 1831, the canal was recognised for the considerable impact it was having on the local economy by Joseph Priestley in his book, Historical Account of the Navigable Rivers, Canals and Railways of Great Britain – *'The advantages of the town of Grantham are very great; corn, timber, coals, lime and many other articles both of import and export, by the communication opened through the canal with those of Nottingham and Cromford, are now transferred at a comparatively easy cost, giving amongst other things, to the inhabitants of this district, the comforts of fuel at a much less expense than heretofore'.*

Sadly, and yet inevitably, the rapid development of the railways from the 1930s onwards brought about a steady decline in the commercial use of the canal. By 1861, the canal was in the hands of the Great Northern Railway, and under the Railway Act of 1921, it was absorbed into the London and North Eastern Group. The canal had been operating at a loss since the 1880s, and although it was still reasonably well used in the early 20th century, its steady decline and, arguably, the neglect of much-needed canal maintenance led to the closure of canal traffic in 1929. The final abandonment of the canal came under the London and North Eastern Railway Act of 1936.

Night Soil

If we take into consideration the growing population of Nottingham throughout the 19th century, the by-product of horsepower and the masses of dispensed or lost accoutrements that flourished in the wake of industrial and commercial growth, then we have a feasible explanation as to why our little buttons ended up on the fields. They arrived via cart from the canal barges that had collected the steaming loads of night soil from Nottingham during the 19th century, right up until the closure of the Grantham Canal in 1929.

So, why was it so important to get the poo out of Nottingham?

Here are some written accounts that might help us understand why the transport of night soil out of Nottingham was of great importance.

H. Taylor, Surgeon, wrote on the 23rd March 1841 – *'The privies, which give rise to a most impure atmosphere; some of them are to a great extent uncovered and give rise to the most filthy effluvia. I can bear witness to many cases of fever which have sprung up in the immediate neighbourhood of the privies, and spread fearfully; and that frequently we have found it advisable and necessary to have the cases removed to the Union for more pure air. I have attended in rooms placed immediately over privies, and where, as might be expected, fever has dwelt with the inmates.'*

In a report written in 1841, J.R. Martin explores the living conditions in and around the crowded courts, alleys and lanes in Nottingham – *'The courts are noisome, narrow, unprovided with adequate means for the removal of refuse, ill-ventilated, and wretched in the extreme, with a gutter or a surface drain running down the centre; they have no back yards, and the privies are common to the whole court; altogether they present scenes of a deplorable character, and of surprising filth and discomfort. In all these confined quarters, too, the refuse matter is allowed to accumulate, until by its mass and its advanced putrefaction, it shall have acquired value as manure; it is thus sold and carted away by the 'muck majors', as the collectors of manure are called in Nottingham.'*

Mr Martin goes on to write – *'The average age at death of the inhabitants of several of the Nottingham districts is only **14** or **15** years, a lower rate than has yet been ascertained to exist in any other city, or within the British Empire.'*

That is a sobering statement indeed!

Picture the night soil being loaded onto barges just off London Road, where Queens Road crosses the canal towards the modern-day incinerator, and imagine the smell and the state of the people who were doing the loading. Our buttons would have been amongst those cargoes. Those people who were doing the loading would most certainly have required a wash if indeed they had access to any bathing facilities that we now take for granted.

That explains the buttons' journey onto the fields, but it tells us very little about what they are, who made them and, most importantly, the lives of the people who used them.

These are their stories…

Richard Pincott
2025
The Field Detectives

NOTTINGHAM TAILORS

ALEXANDER – NOTTINGHAM
THEOBALD ALEXANDER
c. 1854 – 1931
66 LONG ROW & ST PETER'S SQUARE

The founder of Alexander the Great Tailors was Jacob Alexander, a Jewish tailor and clothier from Sandberg in the province of Posen in Prussia, Germany, which is now part of Poland. He brought his wife, Fannie, and his family over to England in about 1873. They then settled in Hanley, Staffordshire, where he set up a tailoring business. By the time he died in 1887, he had left a small empire of tailoring shops to his three sons. Adolph ran the shops in Piccadilly, London, and Hanley while Isaac was in Leicester, and Theobald ran the Nottingham shop.

Theobald was born in about 1854, and his shop was initially situated at 66 Long Row. The shopfront was adorned with *'Alexander the Great'* in enormous letters. Later, the building was incorporated into the Debenham's department store, which closed down in 2021. Next door used to be the Mikado Café, and during the 1920s, it was a venue for many dances and parties. The building was visually striking at this period but is now sadly replaced with a modern block. During Theobald's time, the Mikado may have been the George & Dragon pub.

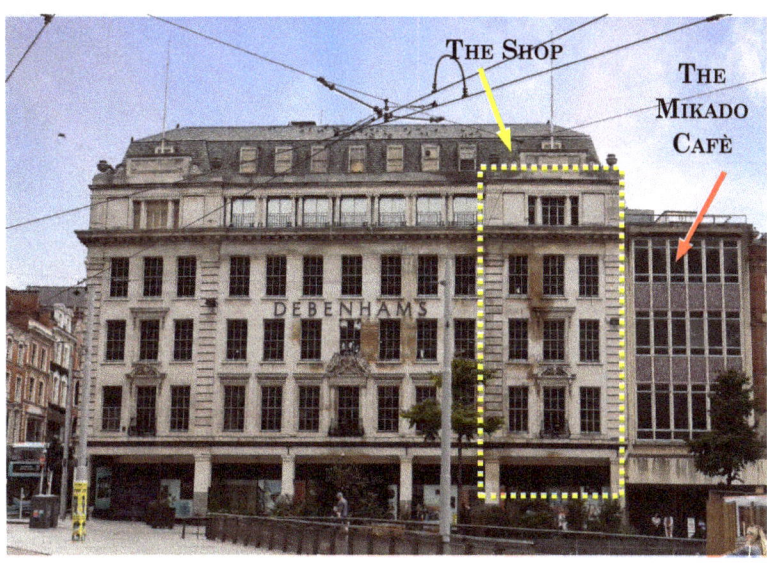

THE EMPTY DEBENHAMS STORE IN 2025

On 6 May 1880, a report in the Nottingham Evening Post revealed that Theobald had been the victim of theft:

> ROBBING DRAPERS. Richard, alias Robert, Tattershaw, alias James Pendle, was charged on remand with stealing a coat, the property of Theobald Alexander, clothier, Long Row, on the 28th of April. The prisoner was further charged with stealing a coat, the property of Messrs. Dixon and Parker, Lister-gate. He pleaded guilty and was sentenced to six months' imprisonment.

A few years later, in 1894, an advertisement in the Nottingham Evening Post announced that Alexander the Great was moving to more extensive premises on the corner of Exchange Walk and St Peter's Square, Nottingham.

Artist Impression of Alexander the Great's Shop at St Peter's Square c. 1890
Artist – Roger Whitehead

Theobald married Adelaide Barnard in 1884 in London, and they had four children: Sonder Barnard (1887), known as Cyril, Daniel Victor (1889), known as Victor, Amelia Doris (1893), known as Millicent, all born in Nottingham, and Leonard Vincent (1900), born in Hampstead, London.

Working through the Nottingham Trade Directories, the shop at 5 St Peter's Square was managed by H. Welburn Pulham by 1904, with Theobald also having premises at 44 West End Lane, London. In the 1912 Kelly's Directory, a tailor named Edward Laws was recorded at the shop and continued there until at least 1925. In the 1941 Kelly's Directory, the premises had been taken over by the famous Montague Burton Ltd – tailors.

By the 1911 census, Theobald had moved to 41 Lansdown Place, Hove, Sussex. From a newspaper article in the London Evening Standard dated 20 January 1912, we learn that Theobald appeared at a Divisional Court charged with *'failure to give an outworker a written or printed statement of the particulars of the rate of wages applicable to the work entrusted to him as required by Section 116 of the Factory Act of 1901'*. Theobald is reported as trading in different parts of London as Alexander the Great, tailor and outfitter. The appeal was dismissed.

Theobald's brother, Adolph, who ran the London stores, was also known for founding the Channel Swimming Club in 1906, with prizes awarded for the encouragement of long-distance sea swimming. This trophy was commissioned and purchased by Adolph for the club in 1912, costing £1200 *(equivalent in 2025 = £160,200)*.

THE ALEXANDER CHANNEL CUP

A very disturbing event occurred in 1926 when Theobald and Adelaide were having dinner at their house, The Palms, Woodchurch Road, in West Hampstead. A thief climbed into a window on the first floor and made off with a haul of jewellery valued at over £1000 *(equivalent in 2025 = £78,280)*. The raid was a matter of only a few minutes, and the man and a woman accomplice drove off in a car. One of the stolen items of jewellery was a necklace with over 100 graduated pearls and set with a diamond clasp.

Theobald died on 31 March 1931 at the age of 76, leaving an estate of a gross value of £57,049 *(equivalent in 2025 = £5,228,000)*. He left £500 to the Jewish Hospital in London to endow a cot in his name and £100 each to various other hospitals, including the Nottingham General Hospital. Theobald and Adolph died within a few days of each other, and a memorial service was held as a tribute to *'Hanley Jewish Benefactors'*, marking their fine example of citizenship. The Alexander brothers emphasised the truth that to be a real Jew was to be a man with a heart and mind for all good causes, irrespective of race, creed or denomination. They possessed the true citizen spirit, and it was rare to find men with so intense a love for their own town.

The timeline for Theobald's button ranges from the 1880s to 1929, when the Grantham Canal closed to traffic.

All money equivalents throughout are calculated at www.measuringworth.com

A Barnfield – Nottingham

Alfred Barnfield
1821 – 1880
&
Alfred Barnfield
1854 – 1906

South Parade

This story begins in Cam, Gloucestershire, where Alfred Barnfield was born on 25 November 1821 and baptised on 25 August 1822 at Dursley Congregational Church the son of worsted maker Jonathon Barnfield and Elizabeth. The first encounter with Alfred in Nottingham was in the 1851 census, where he is recorded as a draper's assistant to Richard Henson at 3 Poultry Arcade. By the 1861 census, Alfred had his own shop at 19 South Parade and was recorded as a merchant tailor, employing two assistants. He is listed in both the 1864 White's and 1869 Morris & Co's Directories, but then in the 1876 Post Office Directory, the entry reads *'Alfred and Alfred Barnfield'*. Not a printing error because the second Alfred was his nephew and his uncle's assistant.

On 23 February 1866, a robbery was reported in the Nottinghamshire Guardian:

> ROBBERY ON THE SOUTH PARADE.—On Monday at the Borough Police Court a middle-aged man, names James Armstrong, was charged with stealing a coat of the value of 22s. 6d *(equivalent in 2025 = £140.60)* from the shop door of Mr. Barnfield, tailor and draper, South Parade. A police-constable, who was near prosecutor's shop on Saturday evening, observed a crowd round the door, and on going to the shop he found prisoner had stolen coat and he took him into custody.—Mr Alfred Barnfield stated that about a quarter past six o'clock on Saturday evening a stall-keeper informed him that the prisoner had stolen a coat from his shop door and had gone up the Poultry. Prisoner was followed, and the coat was found in his possession.—In reply to the magistrates the prisoner stated that he had come from Wolverhampton, and that he obtained a livelihood by begging. He was remanded, in order that inquiries might be made with respect to his character.

At the age of 56, Uncle Alfred married Alice Reader on 6 February 1877 at All Saints Church, Nottingham, and their daughter, Florence Maude, was born in 1878. Sadly, Alfred never had the chance to see his daughter grow up, as he died on 24 February 1880, aged 59. Soon after, on 28 May 1880, the family home was advertised for sale in the Nottingham Guardian, and the auction took place on 15 June 1880. The house was described as – *The freehold detached family residence known as Marlborough House, Elm Avenue, together with Pleasure Garden in front and large kitchen Garden in the rear, planted with choice fruit trees and shrubs, containing an area, including the site of the building, of 2,149 square yards. The House contains, on the Ground Floor, Dining room, with bay, 20ft by 14ft; a Dining room with bay 18ft 6 in. by 13ft; Breakfast room 10ft by 12ft; large Kitchen, Scullery, Larder, China Closet and Butler's Pantry. There are Two Staircases, Six Lofty Bedrooms, Dressing room, Bathroom and w.c. At the rear, there are Coachhouse, Two-stall Stable with Hay Loft, Washhouse, Coalhouse and other Outbuildings, Adjoining the House is a large Conservatory, with an entrance from the Drawing room. The situation is one of the most pleasant and convenient in the town.*

The pleasant and convenient situation was on Cranmer Street in Mapperley Park and has since been demolished and replaced with modern apartments.

Following his uncle's death, Alfred continued to trade alone for the next couple of years. He was born in 1854 in Wooton-under-Edge, Gloucestershire, the son of John Barnfield, a woollen cloth weaver, and Jane Thayers. Alfred married Eleanor Sidoneia Sutton on 17 January 1880 at St Barnabas Roman Catholic Church and continued to be listed in both the 1881 and 1883 Kelly's Directories. However, it would seem that all was not well business-wise, as reported in the Nottinghamshire Guardian on 15 September 1882:

> **ANOTHER FAILURE IN NOTTINGHAM** – In the Bankruptcy Department of the Nottingham County Court a petition for liquidation or composition by arrangement has been filed by Mr Alfred Barnfield, South Parade, Nottingham, tailor and outfitter. Mr Brittle was the solicitor acting for the debtor and obtained from the Registrar an order restraining a suing creditor from proceeding further until after the matter had been before the Court. It is stated that the cause of the failure was that Mr Barnfield found it impossible to meet the demands of certain pressing creditors through inability to collect money owing to him. When this is done by the process of the Court, however, it is expected that a very large dividend will be declared – possibly 20s in the pound. The liabilities are estimated at £750. There is no estimate of assets.

From here on, Alfred's life seemed to decline. In the 1891 census, he had returned to Cam and lived with his parents, but in the 1901 census, he lived alone in Cam, working from home as a tailor. He appears to be separated from his wife, Eleanor, who stayed in Nottingham and had a son in 1902 with Andrew Moloney, a tailor from Ireland. Eleanor died in 1920.

As for Alfred, it went from bad to worse. On 8 April 1904, he was admitted as a pauper to the County Lunatic Asylum in Wotton, and he died there in 1906 at the age of 51. His cause of death was recorded as general paralysis, which is an overarching expression used to describe the death of a person deemed to be insane.

The timeline for the button would have been from the 1860s to 1882.

F W Beet – Nottingham
Frederick William Beet
1849 – 1892
34 Market Street

And he took 'em down with him!

In 1871, London was home to 38,300 tailors, and amongst this multitude, Frederick William Beet can be found working as a draper's assistant at 1-6 Marylebone Lane with 68 other shopmen, apprentices and draper's assistants.

While in London, Frederick married Bertha de Vere Gibson on 26 May 1872, in St Marylebone. Their son, George Henry Frederick Beet, arrived on 8 September 1872 – a somewhat speedy marriage. George was baptised at Battersea Christ Church on 12 January 1873, and their place of abode at this time was 8 Lavender Road, London.

Frederick hailed from Bingham in Nottinghamshire and was born on 6 June 1849, the son of tailor John Beet and Elizabeth Hallam. John continued his tailoring business in Bingham, while Frederick made his way to London. Sometime after his marriage to Bertha, they returned to Nottingham, and this interesting entry can be seen in the Nottingham and District Morris & Co Directory 1877:

Six years later, in 1883, Alfred Monarch Kino, aka Kennard, was bankrupt. It was reported as a heavy failure in the newspapers, with his liabilities stated at £60,000 *(equivalent in 2025 = £8,151,000)*.

> ALFRED MONARCH KINO, tailor, 40 Cornhill, 87 Regent Street, 46 and 47 Lombard Street, E.C. London; Show Rooms, 24 Market Street – F W Beet, manager, attends every Friday, Saturday and Monday.

But back to Frederick Beet…

He had three more children with Bertha: Cecilia Frances (1876), Ethel (1878) and Frederick Newton (1880). Their address in the 1881 census was 13 Gill Street, Nottingham. Sadly, Bertha died in 1881 at the age of only 32 years. With four young children to raise, Frederick soon married again to Eliza Fox on 2 February 1882 at St Mark's Church, and in the 1891 census, they were living at 48 Dune Street.

So, how was business faring?

The 1881 & 1883 Kelly's Directory of Nottingham lists Frederick William Beet & Co, tailor & woollen draper, at 38 Market Street, with the number changing to number 34 in the 1885 Wright's Directory. However, all was not well, as revealed in the Stamford Mercury on 4 March 1887:

> **Bankruptcy**
>
> *(From the London Gazette)*
> *Receiving Orders*
> Beet Frederick William (trading as F.W. Beet and Co.) of Nottingham, tailor.

Then, reported in the Nottinghamshire Guardian on 11 March 1887:

> **THE AFFAIRS OF A NOTTINGHAM TAILOR**
>
> The first meeting of the creditors of Frederick William Beet, of 7 Goldsmith Street and 34 Market Street, Nottingham, tailor, carrying on business as F. W. Beet and Co. was held on Monday at the office of the Official Receiver (Mr H. R. Thorpe) High Pavement, Nottingham. The statement of affairs showed that the amount owing to unsecured creditors was £3,668 8s 4d to creditors fully secured, £4,677 other liabilities, £192; and preferential creditors, £12 10s, total, £8,549 *(equivalent in 2025 = £1,201,000)*. Deducting the total of his assets, left a deficiency of £1001 4s 8d *(equivalent in 2025 = £140,900)*. The causes of the failure were stated as "being pressed and sued by creditors and inability to collect accounts."

There were some discrepancies in the partnership books over money received from his mother-in-law, Mrs Fox, before the dissolution of Beet's partnership with Amos Fox in February 1885. A further newspaper article on 20 December 1888 reported that George Fox was also declared bankrupt. The causes of his failure, amongst others, were assigned by the debtor *to "losses by becoming surety for the payment of the composition to the creditors of his son-in-law, Frederick William Beet."*

George and Amos Fox were brothers.

Another gentleman, George Frederick Slight of the Griffin Inn, also fell foul of becoming a joint surety for Beet and became liable for £1,600 in 1889 *(equivalent in 2025 = £238,500)*. Mr Slight said he had a balance of £3000 to show, and the committee of inspection felt that the debtor had been very unfortunate. But for his suretyship, he would never have been in this position. His Honor suspended the debtor's discharge for three months.

Frederick William Beet died at 28 Great Freeman Street on 2 September 1892 at the age of 42. The cause of death was a combination of diabetes and pneumonia. His wife, Eliza, was present at his death. His profession at the time of his death was a *'tailor traveller'*, another expression for a travelling salesman. No probate record for him can be found, and his disastrous business failure not only cost Frederick dearly but also his family and friends.

Eliza Beet, née Fox, married for a second time to an older man named James Parrott, a publican, on 15 January 1896 at St Mark's. The pub they lived in was called 'The Moulder's Arms' and situated on Bovill Street, Radford.

Further sadness befell the Beet family when Frederick's youngest daughter died. Her death announcement in the Nottingham Evening Post read:

> On the 11 December 1893, after a short but painful illness, Ethel, youngest daughter of the late lamented Frederick William Beet, aged 16 years. Her end was peace. Interred in the Church Cemetery, on Thursday, at three o'clock.

His older daughter, Cecelia Frances, was recorded in the 1891 census as an apprentice milliner, living at 243/4 High Street, Exeter, Devon, with 38 other apprentices and silk mercer assistants. On 4 August 1900, she married a draper named Lawrence Turner in Bath, Somerset, and in the 1911 census, they were living in Acton, Brentford, with their daughters, Pauline Frances and Margaret Ethel de Vere Turner.

In the 1901 census, the eldest son, George Henry Frederick, can be found in Balsall Heath, King's Norton, in Warwickshire, lodging with a family, and his occupation is recorded as a tailor. He married Lilian Reynolds the same year, and in the 1911 census they were living in Northfield, King's Norton. He named his son Frederick Leonard de Vere Beet.

The youngest son, Frederick Newton Beet, remained in Nottingham and became a butcher. In the 1901 census, he was at 7 Ossington Street, living with George Fox, his stepmother's father, and recorded as his nephew.

In the 1911 census, he resided at 175 Radford Road, still with George Fox, but Frederick was now married to Annie Evelyn Loasby. Their daughter is named Margaret de Vere Beet. It would seem that Cecilia, George and Frederick all wanted to keep their mother's middle name in the family.

A somewhat sad and sorry tale of a tailor whose button would have been in use from around 1877 to 1887.

THE SHOP WAS THE SOUVLAKI IN 2025

The building was erected in 1879, so it must have been new when Frederick moved in.

JAMES BELL
1869 – 1957
14 PELHAM STREET

James, a Scotsman, was born on 11 February 1869 in Annan, Dumfries, the son of farmer James Bell and Janet Blackstock. He first appeared in Nottingham in the 1891 census, at the age of 22, where he was living with his uncle, Andrew Armstrong Blackstock, and his cousin, Herbert Renwick Blackstock, at 7 Park Row, Nottingham. All three men were draper travellers.

So it appears that James was introduced to the drapery business at a young age and established his own tailor's shop in 1894, at 14 Pelham Street, Nottingham. The shop remained at this address into the early 2000s. One of the earliest advertisements for his clothing appeared in the Nottingham Evening Post on 24 July 1914:

His early days as a salesman surely paid off with this advertisement:

The Nottingham Evening Post

JAMES BELL is featuring a very high-class ready-for-wear, dust-proof and rain-proof overcoat, designed cut and made by an exclusive west-end house.

The style of this coat is above reproach, and it is stocked in sizes to fit most figures. Price three guineas.

JAMES BELL
14 PELHAM ST.

The Nottingham Evening Post
8 December 1924

JAMES BELL

I do not advertise to tell you that I am a tailor – most people know – but at the moment I have something of real importance to offer you in the way of SUITS AND OVERCOATS at 33% to 50% off this year's prices. See windows or better still come inside and examine the cloths on offer.

14 Pelham Street,
NOTTINGHAM.
'PHONE 3419

On 2 September 1896, James married Florence Holehouse at St Nicholas Church, Nottingham. In the 1901 census, they were recorded living at 1 Patrick Road, West Bridgford, with their son Colin (1897), and by the 1911 census, the family had moved to a large detached house named *'Mount Annan'* at 16 Albemarle Road in Woodthorpe.

World War I broke out, and tragically, Colin was killed. A fate shared by thousands more families. The Roll of Honour for Nottinghamshire reads: *Second Lieutenant Colin Bell originally enlisted and served with service number 67176 as a private in the Sherwood Foresters regiment, he was commissioned as 2nd Lieutenant and is shown as being attached to the 15th (Bantam) Battalion of The Sherwood Foresters at the time of his death. While with his battalion in the trenches near Elverdinghe, on the night of 29th through to the morning of 30th October 1917, the enemy shelled their trenches. This caused a number of casualties to the battalion in that one officer (2nd Lieut Bell) was killed along with four Other Ranks and one officer and 14 Other Ranks were wounded. His body was never recovered or identified and his name is commemorated at the Tyne Cot Memorial, Belgium.*

Despite the tragedy, business continued. At the outbreak of World War II, James Bell was officially appointed as a War Office military tailor, as were numerous tailors all over the country. The war also created fuel shortages, requiring the Ministry of Defence to make requests to businesses to help appease the crisis. On 3 February 1945, in the Nottingham Evening Post, there was this announcement:

A VITAL WAR MATERIAL.

The Ministry of Fuel and Power have requested the greatest economy in the use of Coal, Gas and Electricity. The saving made by remaining CLOSED ALL DAY ON THURSDAYS would be invaluable to the war effort and to the public. In order to render this service we will not open on THURSDAYS until the crisis has passed.

The list of businesses included James Bell and nine other tailors and outfitters.

The 1939 Register records James as being a retired tailor; however, the business continued as James Bell until it was dissolved on 10 August 2010.

James's retirement apparently earned him the opportunity to pursue his passion for golf. He was a prominent amateur golfer and president of the North Shore Golfing Club in Skegness. He was a member of the North Shore Golfing Club, Skegness, and the Wollaton Park Golf Club, as well as a founding member of both the Nottingham Scottish Golfing Society and the Daybrook Golfing Society.

He was a past provincial grand warden and a member of many lodges.

James passed away peacefully at his home on Albemarle Road on 2 December 1957, aged 88, and he was cremated at Wilford Hill Crematorium. He left effects of £152,122 6s 2d *(equivalent in 2025 = £4,947,000).*

The timeline for James's button ranges from about 1894 to the closure of the Grantham Canal in 1929.

THE SHOP WAS TEMPRELL IN 2025

P Benjamin – Hockley
Phineas Benjamin (Fonseca)
1862 – 1943
24 Hockley

The surnames Benjamin and Fonseca seem to be interchangeable. Phineas was born on 19 November 1862 in London, the son of Jewish tailor Benjamin Benjamin, aka Fonseca, and Leah. The family was first found in Nottingham in the 1871 census, living at 24 Hockley, and so began more than 70 years of trading at this address. By the 1891 census, the family's home address had moved to 5 Curzon Street, and that is where Benjamin Benjamin died on 10 March 1895, aged 76. His son, Phineas, then took over the business.

However, ten years earlier, when Phineas was just a clothier's assistant, an act of bravery earned him a mention in the Nottingham Evening Post on 20 July 1885:

ROBBERY FROM THE PERSON IN NOTTINGHAM

At the Summons Court this morning, before Ald. Goldschmidt and Mr. Starey, George Worthington a powerfully built young man, was brought up in custody charged with having stolen a purse containing 8s 6d from the person of Susannah Tiddiman, who was an elderly woman. It was stated that on July 18th she was in Goose-gate about half-past twelve o'clock. She was carrying a satchel, in which she had her purse containing 8s 6d in silver *(equivalent in 2025 = £57.99)*. The prisoner pushed up against her while she was looking in a shop window, she noticed him put his hand in her satchel and taking out her purse ran off. She called out, "Oh, he has took my purse," and Phineas Benjamin, a clothier's assistant, who had watched the prisoner commit the robbery, followed and overtook him. He held him until P.C Padley came up, and the prisoner, who threw the purse into the roadway, was given into custody. Prisoner admitted the offence but pleaded that trade was so bad he could not get an honest living. He was committed for trial at the Quarter Sessions, having been previously convicted.

WELL DONE PHINEAS!

Before Phineas took over from his father, he was in the newspapers again, this time in not such fortuitous circumstances – in the Nottingham Evening Post:

> ### The Nottingham Evening Post
> **19 October 1892**
>
> Philip Levi, 26 Curzon Street, was summoned for assaulting Phineas Benjamin, 5 Curzon Street, on October 8th. Complainant said the defendant thought he owed him 10s *(equivalent in 2025 = £73.34)* which he did not owe, and on the day in question he came up to him at the Salisbury Club and struck him in the face twice and threatened to knock the life out of him. Mr E James represented the defendant. After hearing evidence on both sides defendant was fined 20s *(equivalent in 2025 = £146.70)*

Phineas eventually settled down and married Rosa Hart, the sixth daughter of Isaac H. Hart of Stockton, at St John's Wood synagogue, London, on 17 December 1902. They had two children: Sydney Benjamin Fonseca (1903) and Doris Benjamin Fonseca (1906), both born in Sneinton Dale, Nottingham.

He continued to trade at 24 Hockley but first lived at 10 Victoria Villas, Sneinton Dale, and by the 1912 Kelly's Directory, his home was listed at 30 Hampden Street.

The 1921 census finds Phineas and Rosa in West Bridgford living at 96, Chaworth Road. Their son, Sydney, is recorded working for Phineas as a tailor's cutter, and his daughter, Doris, is performing home duties.

By the time of the 1939 Register, Phineas had retired and was still living on Chaworth Road with Rosa and Doris, who was now a ladies' hairdresser.

At the age of 75, Rosa died, and her death was reported in the Nottingham Journal on 5 March 1940 as:

> ### First Jewish burial at Wilford Hill
> The first burial in a new Jewish cemetery adjoining Wilford Hill, took place yesterday. The cemetery was recently consecrated by the Chief Rabbi, the Very Rev. Dr Joseph Herman Hertz, of the United Hebrew College, London.
>
> The burial was that of Mrs Rosa Fonseca, better known as Mrs Rosa Benjamin, who lived in Nottingham for 50 years. Her husband and his father traded at 24, Hockley for more than 70 years.

So, what happened to the children?

Doris's life was sadly cut short at the age of 36. She died at the General Hospital, Nottingham, on 26 September 1942, and at the time of her death, she had been living at 160 Musters Road, West Bridgford. She left effects of £868 13s *(equivalent in 2025 = £54,600)*.

Her brother, Sydney, moved to Birmingham, and he married Lily Silverstone in 1932. The couple had two children: Colin Gerald Fonseca (1933) and Valerie Kay Fonseca (1938), and they lived at 25 Staplehurst Road, Birmingham. However, in the 1939 Register, only Sydney was at home and recorded as a tailor's cutter and also special constable R523. In the Birmingham City Police records he was described as 5 ft 9½ inches tall, with a fresh complexion, dark hair, brown eyes and a birthmark on his right cheek.

When WWII broke out, an incredible story unfolded. Sydney's wife and children made their way aboard the *SS Baltrover* on 20 August 1940, heading for Boston, Massachusetts, USA, as war refugees. Colin was seven, and Valerie was only two years old. Colin was described as 4 ft tall, having a fair complexion with brown eyes and auburn hair, and he had £10 with him *(equivalent in 2025 = £736.50)*. The family stayed in the USA for four years, arriving back in England aboard the *Mauretania* on 22 May 1944.

Phineas died on 18 December 1943, aged 81, at the Selly Oak Hospital, Raddlebarn Road, although his home address was 25 Staplehurst Road, Hall Green, Birmingham, his son's house. However, his funeral took place at Wilford Hill Cemetery, Nottingham, where he is buried with his wife, Rosa. Phineas left effects of £2015 13s 6d *(equivalent in 2025 = £122,300)*.

The timeline for his button would be between 1895 and 1929.

HEADSTONE AT THE JEWISH CEMETERY, WILFORD HILL
OF
PHINEAS AND ROSA FONSECA
The headstone of their daughter, Doris, lies close by.

Special thanks to Neil Pike for allowing us entry to the Jewish Cemetery to take photographs.

T BIRD – NOTTINGHAM

THOMAS BIRD
1855 – 1899

3 GOLDSMITH STREET

THE LOVE BIRDS

This button tells a poignant story of love and loss. Thomas Bird was born on 20 February 1855 in Lancaster, Lancashire, the son of Mary Bird née Robinson, a widow; his father is unknown. Thomas's baptism took place at the Fulwood Barracks Chapel on 13 April 1855. Mary would have been about 46 years old when Thomas was born.

Mary had a curious life. At about the age of 18, she married tailor William Bird on 26 July 1826 in Leeds. They had a son, Isaac (1827), and a daughter, Margaret (1835), both born in Lancaster. Tragically, William died of consumption and was buried on 1 May 1836, at Christ Church, Hulme, Lancashire, aged only 26 years old. Mary gave birth to another daughter, Elizabeth, on 22 February 1837. It is doubtful she would have known she was pregnant when her husband died.

Now, here is where the curiosity begins.

Her next son, William Robinson Bird, was born in 1839, and his baptism records his father as tailor William Bird. He had been dead for three years. John was the next child who was born around 1845, but there is no record of him being baptised. Richard Pye Bird followed, and his baptism took place at the Fulwood Barracks Chapel on 19 March 1850. His mother was recorded as Mary, a widow, but there is no father's name. It might be a coincidence, but there was a lodger named John Pye living with the Birds at 10, Custom House Alley, Lancaster. Two and two could be put together here, but on his marriage certificate, Richard names his father as John Bird, a gardener.

Next came Thomas, our tailor of interest in Nottingham. According to the census returns, he lived at various addresses in Lancaster – Fleet Street in 1841, Custom House Alley in 1851, George Street in 1861, and Sun Street in 1871, where he is recorded as being 16 years old and an apprentice, but it does not say the nature of his apprenticeship. However, his sister Margaret could provide a clue.

She was 20 years older than Thomas and married to Septimus J'Anson, a tailor, in 1858. Perhaps he was able to help young Thomas enter the tailoring trade.

A love story now unfolds…

Living in the same area as the Birds was a girl named Ellen Elizabeth Collinson. Her family was at St George's Quay in the 1851 census, a stone's throw away from Custom House Alley, where the Birds were living. It is possible they went to school together. They stayed close to each other, and along with Thomas, she was a witness at his brother Richard's wedding in 1874, in Lancaster. Four years later, Thomas and Ellen married in the St George's Square, Hanover district of London in 1878. Seven years later, the couple were living on Tottenham Terrace, Nottingham, where Thomas's occupation was recorded in the 1881 census as a tailor's cutter.

A successful career appeared to be burgeoning for Thomas. He is listed in the 1891 Kelly's Directory of Nottingham as a tailor at 3 Goldsmith Street and continued to trade there, as listed in the 1898-99 Wright's Directory. The couple had moved to Chaworth Road, West Bridgford, in the 1891 census, one of the more affluent areas of Nottingham, and a sign that all was well. Sadly, this was not to be the case. Thomas died on 25 July 1899, at 5 Queens Terrace, Scarborough Avenue, Skegness, Lincolnshire. He left effects of £162 15s 1d *(equivalent in 2025 = £24,710)*.

They had no children, and Ellen continued to live at the same address. In the 1901 census, she was recorded as a lodging house keeper, although the enumerator wrote her as living at 3 Queens Terrace, not number five. Ellen died on 15 October 1908, leaving effects of £554 6s 1d *(equivalent in 2025 = £78,060)*

They are both buried at St Clement Graveyard, Skegness, where the headstone lies as part of the path around the graveyard.

Thomas Bird's button made its way onto a field between about 1880 and 1898.

Thomas & Ellen's headstone
St Clement's Graveyard

Special thanks to Judi Gaskill from the Skegness u3a Local History Group for her research into locating number 5 Queens Terrace..

Carey & Nephew
Carey Parker
Carey Parker & Tirbutt
Nottingham

Francis Carey 1817 – 1883
George Carey Parker 1831 – 1906
Frank Carey Parker 1858 – 1940
Edward Bachelor Tirbutt 1830 – 1906
Corner of Clumber Street & Pelham Street

Image above taken in 1893
The shop was Zara in 2025

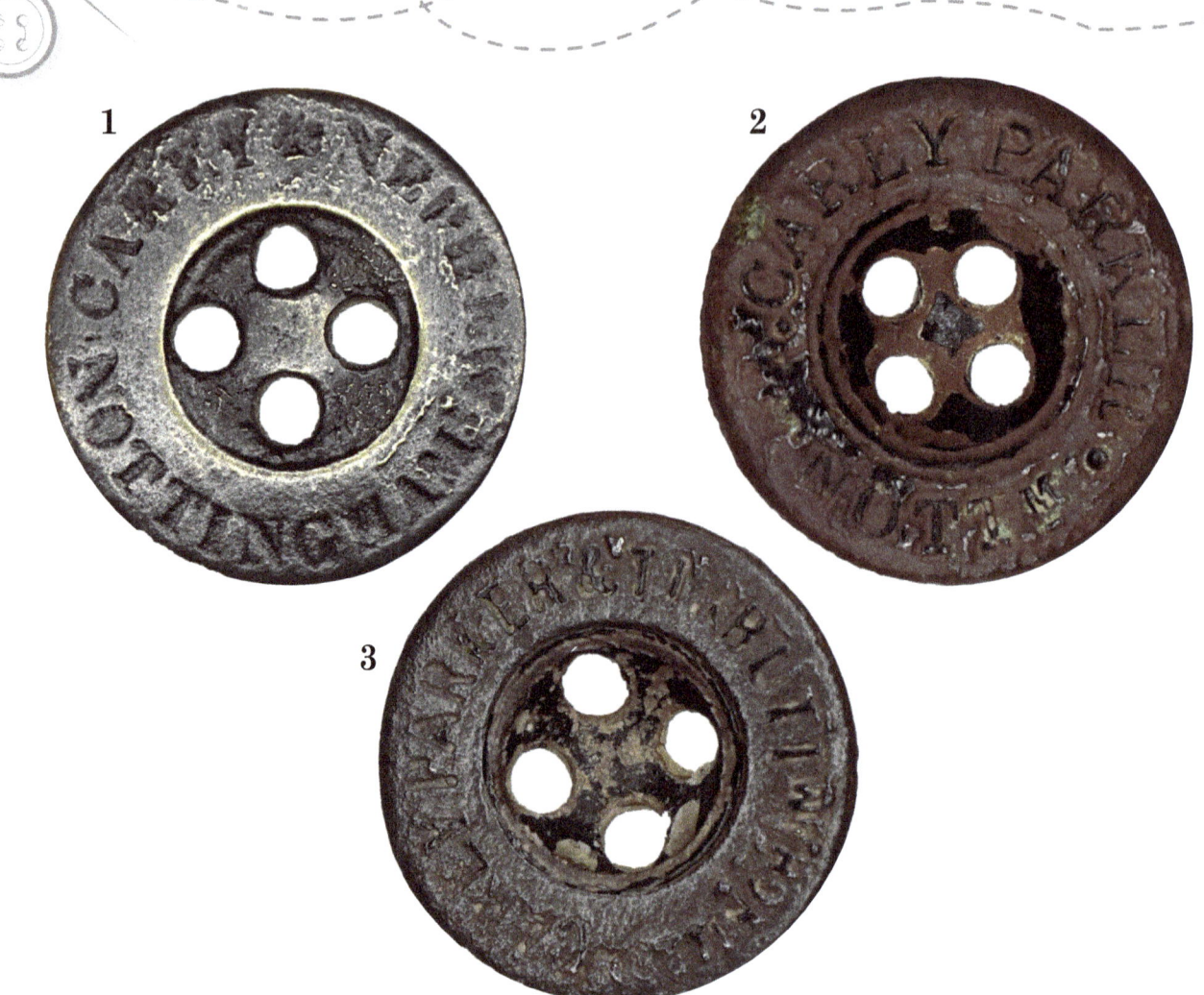

Three buttons feature in the collection, each connected to members of an extended family; they are: 1. Francis Carey & Nephew, 2. F. Carey Parker, 3. Carey Parker & Tirbutt.

Button 1 – Carey & Nephew – can be attributed to Francis Carey and his nephew, Francis Carey Parker. Francis Carey was born in 1817 in Nottingham, and his father, George, already ran a hatters, glovers and furriers business at Clumber House on the corner of Clumber Street and Pelham Street. In the 1832 White's Directory, the firm is listed as George Carey & Son, the son being Francis, who had a lucky escape from serious injury or death before he had taken over from his father. This incident was reported on 26 December 1835 in the Nottingham & Newark Mercury:

> On Wednesday last, as Mr. Francis Carey, son of Mr. Carey, hatter, in this town, was coming down Clumber-street, from Basford, in a gig, when passing the end of Lincoln-street, the pole of a fly belonging to Mrs Morton, of Mansfield, which was coming down Lincoln-street, came in contact with the wheel of Mr. Carey's gig with great force, and broke the spokes of the wheel, and the splash-board, and otherwise injured the gig. Mr. Carey was thrown out on to the pavement, and severely bruised and cut, but we are glad to say his wounds are not dangerous. The horse did not sustain any injury.

Two years earlier, in August 1833, there had been a serious setback to the business when a terrible fire destroyed Carey's warehouse, situated on the south side of St Peter's Gate. Some of the hat makers employed there had been drinking and were playing pranks on each other while Mr Carey was out of town. A resulting scuffle led to a spillage of inflammable chemicals that ignited. The fire spread rapidly, but the offenders escaped with only burns to their legs. A woman working upstairs had to be rescued, and the complete stock of furs and materials went up in flames. Firefighters were called, and it took three hours to put out the blaze. Tragically, a builder named Benjamin Lucas, who was extremely active throughout, fell through a roof, fracturing his skull. The poor young man died the following day.

Fortunately for Mr Carey, he was insured, and business continued, with Francis taking over from his father in 1838. However, by 1842, Francis was declared bankrupt, although he remained in business. In 1857 Francis went into partnership with his nephew, George Carey Parker, creating Carey & Nephew, hatters, furriers, tailors, outfitters and hosiers, and in the 1864 White's Directory of Nottingham, they appear under outfitters and hatters.

George Carey Parker was born in 1831 in Loughborough, Leicestershire, the son of William Parker and Eliza Carey (Francis's sister). George married Ellen Selina Peel, and by the 1861 census, they were living on Addison Street Esplanade, Sherwood, with their two children, Francis Carey Parker, born on 21 June 1858, and Anne (1859). George's uncle Francis was not far away on Cavendish Hill.

By the 1871 census, George and his family were living at 8 Norfolk Terrace, Fulham, London, with George now recorded as a commercial traveller. The Nottingham shop was now in Francis Carey's name alone. George and Ellen remained in the London area, and George died in 1906 in St Albans. Meanwhile, their son, Francis, known as Frank, returned to Nottingham in about 1881 and went into partnership with Francis Carey, his great-uncle, becoming Carey & Parker.

Frank married Mary Elizabeth Harvey on 22 February 1881 at Southwell Minster. They had eight children: Mabel Ellen (1881), George Francis (1884), Frank Harvey (1887), Reginald Peet (1890), Elsie Mary (1892), Sidney Edward Carey (1894), Winifred Anna (1897), and Ernest Richard (1905).

The partnership of Carey & Nephew was dissolved on 8 March 1883 following Francis's death. He left effects of £468 12s *(equivalent in 2025 = £63,660)*. Frank took over and was listed as Frs. Carey Parker, hatter, tailor & outfitter in the 1885 Wright's Directory – **Button 2 – F. Carey Parker.**

At some point after this, Frank partnered up with Edward Bachelor Tirbutt, and the business became F. Carey Parker & Tirbutt, as featured on **Button 3 – Carey Parker & Tirbutt.**

The pair were busy doing good deeds in town, as reported on 25 August 1890 in the Nottingham Evening Post, where Carey Parker & Tirbutt are amongst a list of businesses donating battalion prizes to the Robin Hood Rifles.

Indeed, in the Nottingham Guardian on 20 April 1889, this advertisement was placed:

> MILITARY Tailors Wanted (outdoor). — Apply at once, Carey Parker and Tirbutt, Clumber-street, Nottingham.

Also this one in the Nottingham Evening Post on 25 June 1889:

> CAREY PARKER AND TIRBUTT
>
> TAILORS, HATTER, AND OUTFITTER
>
> SOLE AGENTS FOR
> PRITCHARD'S PRIZE MEDAL
> SILK AND FELT HATS,
> IN THE
> LATEST LONDON STYLES
>
> CLUMBER STREET, NOTTINGHAM

Despite their efforts together, the partnership was relatively short-lived and was dissolved by mutual consent on 27 March 1893.

Following the split with Edward Tirbutt, Frank went into partnership with Hervey Jones and William Robert Oliver, and they were placing advertisements in the newspapers, such as this one in the Newark Advertiser on 13 November 1895:

> **CAREY PARKER & CO.,**
> Civil, Military, and Clerical Tailors and Outfitters
> **AUTUMN & WINTER SEASON**
> SPECIALITIES.
>
> BLACK MORNING COAT & VEST, in Unfaced Shetland Twills........ From £8 8s. 0d.
> BEAUTIFUL SOFT CASHMERE DRESS JACKET & VEST, Silk
>   Facings and Collar.. From £8 10s. 0d.
> OUR "SPECIAL" CASHMERE DRESS SUIT.................................. From £4 14s. 6d.
> THE CHESTERFIELD OVERCOAT in all the Newest Materials........ From £2 17s. 0d
> OUR WELL-MADE, SMART, BUSINESS SUITS, made from a Grand
>   Selection of Scotch Cheviots .... From £8 3s. 0d.
> OUR GUINEA TROUSERS IN AN IMMENSE VARIETY OF NEW DESIGNS
>
> **CLUMBER STREET, NOTTINGHAM**

In both the 1902 and 1905 Wright's Directories, the firm was still Carey Parker & Co., but the shop had moved to 7 The Poultry, Nottingham, and was now offering ladies' tailoring. The move to The Poultry took place in about 1900.

Once again, Francis's alliance with Jones and Oliver was short, with the company being dissolved on 5 September 1906 and acquired by Messrs Porter & Co (see page 72), who moved the business to 47 Clumber Street.

By the 1911 census, Frank had relocated to Cheshire and lived at 37 School Lane, Sale; his occupation is recorded as tailor & outfitter. That same year, Frank was declared bankrupt and reported in the Edinburgh Gazette on 23 May 1911.

He continued to work as a tailor's salesman and ended his days living with his daughter, Winifred, at 43 Willow Way, Manchester. By now, he was widowed, and he died on 2 May 1940, aged 81. No probate record can be found for him.

Although his business ended unsuccessfully, Frank had been an upstanding citizen while he lived in Nottingham. During his time in Southwell, he became honorary secretary of the Southwell Horticultural and Cottage Gardening Society. Also, in June 1890, he co-founded the St Mary's Masonic Lodge, Southwell, which is now on Goldsmith Street in Nottingham. He was churchwarden at St Saviour's Church, and in 1896, he gifted a beautiful stained glass window to the church. It can be found in the north aisle and is a legacy that can still be seen today.

EDWARD BACHELOR TIRBUTT

Although the Parker-Tirbutt partnership was brief, Edward Tirbutt's story is integral to their button's history.

He was born in 1830 and baptised on 21 July 1833 at Michaelchurch, Herefordshire, with his brother John Bachelor Tirbutt and his sister Sarah Bachelor Tirbutt, the children of farmer Thomas Tirbutt and Susan Bachelor. Sadly, their mother died in 1836 and was buried on 1 May at Michaelchurch. Following her death, the children appear to have been separated from their father, as in the 1841 census, Edward and John were found living with their uncle, William Bachelor, a tailor and draper on Broad Street, Worcester, while their sister, Sarah, was living with a schoolmistress in Kempsey, Worcestershire. Sarah's life was cut short at the age of 19, and her burial took place on 3 June 1854 at St Thomas's Church, Birmingham.

In the 1851 census, Edward, now a tailor and draper, was found as a visitor in the household of William Caldicot at 10 Easy Row, Claines, Worcester. His brother, John, was lodging there and recorded as a professor of music. He went on to live in Bromsgrove, Worcestershire, where he died aged 65 on 9 September 1897.

Now, back to Edward.

In Slater's General & Classified Directory of Birmingham 1852-3, he is listed as a tailor and draper at 18 Ann Street, Birmingham; his house was on Latimer Street South. By August 1853, Edward had declared himself bankrupt and was incarcerated in Coventry Gaol. However, a merchant or trader could avoid debtor's prison by declaring themselves bankrupt if they owed less than £100, but it would cost them £10 for the privilege *(in 1853, the equivalent in 2025 = £1,365)*.

How Edward paid his debts or was bailed out is unknown.

He then made a fleeting appearance in Nottingham, where he married Elizabeth Mary Lee on 17 March 1855 at St Stephen's Church, Sneinton, and resurfaced in the historical records in Dublin, Ireland, where their children were born. Sadly, there was also a burial for a baby girl, Alice Lee, on 10 May 1858, aged 0, and another on 18 February 1861 for Edward Robert, aged 0. However, the surviving children were Marion Arden (c. 1858), Catherine (c. 1864), Ellen (c. 1865), Lilian (1866), Edward George (1868), William (1869), and Francis Edward (1871).

Edward is listed in Thom's Irish Almanac and Official Directory of the United Kingdom of Great Britain and Ireland 1863 as a merchant tailor at 7 Wicklow Street. Incredibly, in 1866, Edward received the appointment of tailor to His Grace the 2nd Marquis of Abercorn, James Hamilton. He certainly moved up in the world and, within a few months, had moved to 50 Dawson Street. He held this position for at least twenty years.

JAMES HAMILTON
THE 2ND MARQUIS OF ABERCORN

Sadly, his wife, Elizabeth, died on 23 March 1882 and is buried in Deansgrange Cemetery, Dublin. Perhaps her loss prompted Edward's return to England, as in the 1891 census he was recorded living at 188 Goldsmith Street, Nottingham, and had now set up in business with Frank Carey Parker at the Clumber Street shop – Carey Parker & Tirbutt.

As already mentioned, their partnership was dissolved in 1893, and sadly, Edward was recorded in the 1901 census as partially paralysed and living with his daughter, Marion, at 130 Mansfield Road. Perhaps the heartbreak that struck the Tirbutt family a few years earlier had a drastic effect on him when his son, Edward George, died in tragic circumstances. It was reported in the Toronto Daily Mail on 20 July 1889:

> QUEBEC July 17th, at Quebec, Canada, Edward George Tirbutt, the young Englishman removed from the steamship Lake Superior in a dying condition on Tuesday, died yesterday in the Jeffry Hale hospital. He was only 21 years of age and was on his way to Nottingham, England where his father now resides.

He was buried on 20 July 1889 at St Peter's Church, Quebec, Canada.

Further misery hit the family when the eldest son, Francis Edward, died on 18 January 1920 on Quequén beach, Buenos Aires, Argentina, trying to save a drowning swimmer. He was the vice consul in Tucuman, Argentina, and had married Margaret Blanche Lyons in Rosario, Argentina; they had six children.

Edward died on 26 November 1906 in Nottingham, and perhaps it was fortunate that he did not live long enough to learn of a second son's death. No probate record can be found.

The timeline for the three buttons ranges from 1857 to 1906.

A G Carrington – Nottingham
Alfred George Carrington
1859 – 1933
40 Clumber Street

A Torrid Tailor's Tale

Alfred first appeared in the 1888 Kelly's Directory of Nottingham, listed as a tailor and clothier at 40 Clumber Street. The 1891 census records his home address at 46 Forest Road West, an attractive residence at the time, so business must have been flourishing.

Alfred George Carrington was born in 1859, the son of furniture dealer Henry Hugh Carrington and Eliza Sotheran. They had married in 1845, and Alfred's sister, Eliza, was born in 1853. Their father died in 1878, leaving effects of under £2000 *(equivalent in 2025 = £261,800)*, so at least the family was not left destitute.

On 14 May 1891, Alfred married Nellie Annie Mann, who was born on 1 December 1872, the daughter of Thomas Mann, a box manufacturer who lived in The Park, an extremely desirable address. The wedding took place at St Matthew's; Alfred was 29, and Nellie was a mere 18 years of age and pregnant. Their son, Thomas Hugh, was born on 22 November 1891. What emerged from this marriage was not marital bliss but a disturbing account of domestic violence.

After four years of marriage, Nellie filed for divorce on the grounds of cruelty and adultery. Her petition, dated 7 February 1895, describes the horrific outbursts that her husband subjected her to. Shortly after their marriage, Alfred became abusive, assaulting her frequently. Indeed, in October 1891, while Nellie was pregnant, he struck her in the face with his elbow, causing her nose to bleed and blackening her eye. The abuse continued for many months, with Alfred returning home drunk, using abusive and violent language. He accused her of him not being the father of their child, which caused her *'severe mental pain'*. He tried to strangle her, and on another occasion he threw a small oak table and two chairs at her in a drunken rage. He smashed glassware on the table, he kicked her, and he twice threatened to shoot her with a loaded revolver. Nellie's health became so greatly impaired that on 24 April 1893 she left and filed for divorce.

It did not end there. Not only had Alfred been abusing Nellie, but he had also committed adultery with a young woman named Violet Coles in Leicester on about 10 November 1893. Violet was only

16 years old and gave birth to their child, Alfred Henry Carrington, around 10 August 1894, after which they continued to live together as Mr & Mrs Coles at 13 Crescent Street, Leicester.

Nellie's divorce was granted on 3 February 1896, and she was granted 15s a week in maintenance *(equivalent in 2025 = £116.80)*.

> [Decree absolute]
>
> **In the High Court of Justice**
>
> PROBATE, DIVORCE AND ADMIRALTY DIVISION
>
> **(DIVORCE.)**
>
> Before the Right Honourable SIR FRANCIS HENRY JEUNE, KNIGHT,
> The President
> sitting at the Royal Courts of Justice, Strand, in the County of Middlesex,
> On the 3rd day of Feb. 1896
>
> Carrington against Carrington
>
> Referring to the Decree made in this Cause on the 22nd day of July 1895 whereby it was decreed that Marriage had and solemnized on the 14th day of May 1891 at the Parish Church in the parish of St Matthew Nottingham in the County Town of Nottingham between Nellie Annie Carrington then Mann Spinster the Petitioner and Alfred George Carrington the Respondent be dissolve by reason that since the celebration thereof the Said Respondent had been guilty of Adultery & Cruelty Towards the Petitioner
>
> unless sufficient cause be shown to the Court why the said Decree should not be made absolute, within six months from the making thereof—and no such cause having be shown, the President on application of the said Petitioner by his final Decree pronounced and declared the said Marriage to be dissolved.
>
> C A. Musgrove
> Registrar

In the words of the petition, the solicitor *'humbly prays that your lordship will be pleased to decree that your petitioner's marriage with the said Alfred George Carrington may be dissolved, that she may have custody of her child and such further relief as may be just.'*

Nellie had returned home to her parents at 14 Pelham Crescent, The Park, with her son and continued to live there for the next forty years or more.

She eventually remarried at 50 years of age in 1922 to Frederick Pearson, the company director of Pearson's of Nottingham. Nellie died in 1956 at the age of 84, in Nottingham. Her son, Thomas, worked as a display manager at Boots, and when he died in 1972, he was a retired finance company accounts clerk, living at Flat 3, 5 Kenilworth Road, The Park.

Meanwhile, Alfred and Violet made no delay and married in early 1896, as soon as his divorce was finalised. Violet then went to live at Alfred's home on Forest Road West. In the 1901 census, four children were recorded: Alfred Henry (1894), Violet (1896), Victor (1897) and Cyril (1898). Violet's father, Thomas Coles, a retired law stationer, was also living there.

Unbelievably, at the same time Alfred was abusing Nellie, his sister, Eliza, confided in him that she was also being abused by her husband. Eliza filed for divorce on 28 May 1895, and the circumstances described in her petition bore a distinct resemblance to those that Nellie was suffering at the hands of her brother. Eliza's husband was Herbert Renwick Blackstock, also a draper, and they lived with Alfred at Forest Road for a while. Whether they were in business together is uncertain. When the domestic violence was taking place, Herbert and Eliza were living at 20 Shakespeare Villas. Soon after their marriage, Herbert was drinking heavily and acting violently towards Eliza. On one occasion in March 1895, he returned home drunk and quarrelsome, so she refused to sleep with him. She went to the bedroom and locked the door, but Herbert rushed upstairs, broke in the door, seized her, threatened to kill her and throw her, the bed and all her belongings out of the window. Not only that, but Herbert committed adultery at a house of ill fame on Kirkewhite Street with Ann Mitchell, who was employed as a nurse at their house.

Eliza's divorce was granted on 22 June 1896.

Now, back to Alfred… He continued to trade from 40 Clumber Street until the 1912 Wright's Directory, when this address was now occupied by the Paris Millinery Company. Alfred is only listed at his home address in subsequent directories. Alfred and Violet remained married for 37 years until Alfred's death on 25 April 1933, aged 74. Despite his history, the business must have remained buoyant, as he left effects of £11,935 12s 8d *(equivalent in 2025 = £1,143,000)*.

Whether their marriage was a happy one is unknown, but there was a tinge of sadness for them when the eldest son, Alfred, born from the initial adultery, died in 1905 at the age of ten. The youngest son, Cyril, died on 22 April 1919, aged 20, and they are both buried with Violet's father in the General Cemetery, Nottingham. The middle son, Victor, worked with Alfred as a tailor & clothier assistant, but he too died comparatively young in 1932, aged 35. Their daughter, Violet, never married, and she died on 6 December 1948 at Mapperley Hospital, leaving effects of £12698 12s 5d *(equivalent in 2025 = £662,800)*.

Mrs Violet Carrington died suddenly on 23 February 1946, and she is buried at the Church (Rock) Cemetery, Nottingham. From her questionable beginnings, it would seem she became an upstanding woman in the community. She became president of the Sherwood Women's Conservative Association and a keen supporter of the National Boys' Home and the PDSA. The newspaper reported that her daughter, Violet, was unable to attend the funeral due to illness, but her granddaughter, Deidre Carrington, was present.

The timeline for this button ranges from 1888 to 1929.

Dixon & Parker

William Dixon
1833 – 1917
&
Thomas Prosser Parker
1845 – 1927

Nottingham – Various Locations

Dixon & Parker is surely a well-remembered clothing shop by many Nottingham inhabitants. D & P ran from 1864 to 2012, but how did it all start?

The founder, William Dixon, was born in Grantham and baptised on 19 April 1833 at St Wulfram's Church, the son of joiner/carpenter David Dixon and Mary Auger. William had an older brother, John Auger (1831), and a sister, Mary Auger (1836). Sadly, their mother died in 1839 and was buried on 25 March at Spittlegate Wesleyan Methodist Burial Ground. Nonetheless, David remarried soon after to Elizabeth Hillam on 22 July 1839 at Croxton Kerrial, Leicestershire, and they had four children: James (1841), Joseph (1844), Sarah (1847) and Thomas (1849), all born in Grantham.

William cannot be located in the 1851 census; however, a curious entry appeared in Chelsea, London, that might explain matters. John (Auger) Dixon is recorded as aged 19, born in Grantham, whose occupation was an upholsterer's salesman, and he is the correct age for being William's elder brother. With him is James Dixon, aged 17, also born in Grantham, a draper's shopman, and he is the correct age for William. The conclusion drawn for now is that the enumerator recorded William's name incorrectly, as the real James is at home in Grantham.

John Auger disappeared from the available historical records used for this study, and James died from a short illness following his return from Calcutta on 3 November 1860.

As a footnote, Calcutta was said to be the epicentre of cholera in the world – food for thought.

On the other hand, business for William was on the up and up. He married Susannah Woodcock (1835) from Croxton Kerrial, the daughter of veterinary surgeon Benjamin Woodcock. They wed on 16 November 1858 at St Mary's, Leicester, and are recorded in the 1861 census as living on North

Parade, Grantham, with their first son, Arthur (1859). William's occupation was an outfitter, employing two boys. William and Susannah had six more children: John Auger Jnr (1861), Clara (1863), Frederick James (1865), Ada Mary (1867), Emily Woodcock (1869) and Charles Percy (1873), all born in Grantham.

Interestingly, the 1869 Morris's Directory of Nottingham lists William having shops at Carol Gate, Retford, 2 Lister Gate, Nottingham, and 62 Goose Gate, Nottingham, showing that his business had already begun to expand. The 1871 census recorded William living at High Street, Grantham, with his occupation as outfitter (master), employing 12 assistants and numerous apprentices. Soon after, they moved to 13 Gedling Grove, Waverley Street, later known as Annesley Villas.

In the Nottingham Journal on 11 July 1874, notice was given:

> NOTICE
>
> W. DIXON
>
> CLOTHIER AND OUTFITTER,
>
> 3, & 5, LISTER-GATE, NOTTINGHAM,
>
> Having taken into Partnership his manager, Mr THOS. PARKER, the above business will in future be conducted under the style or firm of
>
> DIXON AND PARKER,
>
> Who solicit a continuance of that liberal support which the public has for the last ten years conferred upon this Establishment.

The new partner was Thomas Prosser Parker.

And what better than a cosy new rug in time for Christmas?

> Nottingham Journal 21 December 1874
>
> GREAT SALE of a MANUFACTURER'S STOCK of CARRIAGE AND TRAVELLING RUGS,
> BOUGHT AT A LARGE DISCOUNT,
> FROM COST-PRICE
> DIXON AND PARKER
> LISTER-GATE
> NOTTINGHAM

By Morris's 1877 Directory, the shops are now listed as Dixon & Parker at 3, 5, 7, 9 Lister Gate with W Dixon & Co., Wholesale Juvenile Clothiers, at 35 Houndsgate.

A common occurrence was reported in the Nottingham Journal on 24 June 1876 with headline – THEFTS FROM SHOP DOORS.

The culprit was apprehended and sent to prison for two calendar months with hard labour, with the bench remarking that they considered the practice of hanging goods outside shop doors afforded great temptation to thieves and they were very sorry to see it so much done.

Dixon & Parker continued to boom throughout the 1880s, and in the Nottingham Evening Post on 8 September 1883, the desire to clothe a substantial number of Nottingham men in trousers was advertised:

> "Bench remarking that they considered the practice of hanging goods outside shop doors afforded great temptation to thieves and they were very sorry to see it so much done.."

SPECIAL PURCHASE

TWO THOUSAND PAIRS OF MEN'S TROUSERS

PRICE 4^s 11^D 5^s 11^D 6^s 11^D

DIXON AND PARKER

5 TO 9 LISTER GATE

SEE SHOP WINDOWS

(equivalent prices in 2025 = £33.42, £40.21 and £47.00)

Not only could men now afford trousers, but Dixon and Parker was the go-to place to *'clothe your boys'*, with on average 200 boys weekly being dressed smartly because *'D&P at all times holds one of the largest retail stocks in the country.'*

Tragedy almost struck the Lister Gate shop when a fire broke out in December 1885. It started in the boiler house of the warehouse and *'the brigade set to work from a hydrant and after working some time subdued the fire before serious damage was done. The origin of the fire was attributed to the over heating of a flue, which ignited the roof, this being completely consumed.'*

By 1907, Dixon & Parker Ltd had branches at 1-15 Lister Gate, 3 Long Row & 14 Arkwright Street in Nottingham.

28 & 29 High Street, Birmingham

229 High Street, West Bromwich

22 & 23 Market Place and High Street, Grantham

248 High Street, Lincoln

19 & 20 Stodman Street, Newark

2 & 4 Midland Road, Wellingborough

7 Haymarket, Leicester

Other partners were:

Matthews & Co at 42 & 44 Derby Road and 16 Angel Row, Nottingham (see page 62)

Prosser & Co. at 16 Angel Row, 23 Hockley, 37 St Ann's Well Road, Nottingham, 36 & 38 Main Street, Bulwell, 16 & 22 High Street, Hucknall Torkard and High Street, Kettering

Dixon & Berry at Market Place, Melton Mowbray and Oakham

W. Tarrant at 134 High Street, Putney, London S.W.

Dixon and Parker were well and truly on the map.

In the 1891 census, William and Susannah had moved to Dulwich, Camberwell, London, and were living at Bellevue, 17 Herne Hill. In the 1901 census, William was recorded as living on his own means, and with him were his wife, Susannah, his unmarried daughter, Ada Mary, four servants and a visitor named Susannah Hipwell, a schoolteacher. A trip to Hastings was recorded in the 1911 census, where 77-year-old William and Susannah are staying in a lodging house at 5 Carlisle Parade, along with their daughter, Clara, also unmarried. A trained nurse is also with them.

Susannah died on 20 February 1915, leaving effects of £1200 8s 10d *(equivalent in 2025 = £129,700)*. She was joined by William on 17 July 1917, and he left effects of £33,666 10s 3d *(equivalent in 2025 = £2,545,000)*. Most definitely a rags-to-riches tailor's tale.

Without mentioning William's sons, the Dixon side of the story would remain incomplete. Arthur's life was cut tragically short when he died of gastric fever on 1 December 1876 at the age of 17, in Frankfurt, Germany. There is a dedication to him on a stained glass window commissioned by his father in St Andrew's Church, Nottingham.

Thankfully, the second son, John Auger Jnr, fared far more fortuitously. In the 1871 census, he was at a boarding school at 34 & 36 London Road, Leicester, and later attended Nottingham High School. In subsequent censuses, he is recorded as a clothing manufacturer and became the managing director of Dixon & Parker. He married on 24 October 1910 at St Stephen's, Hyson Green, to one of his young milliners, Maude Beatrice Hannington. She was 24 years his junior, which evidently caused something of a sensation in the family. They had two daughters, Maud Hannington (1911) and Dorothy Margaret (1915).

Another famous connection to Nottingham has to be mentioned here. Maud Hannington Dixon had first married William Herbert Richardson Radford in 1935, but he died in 1937. Maud's second husband was Thomas Kenneth Parr, whom she married in 1938. He founded Pork Farms and its famous pork pie.

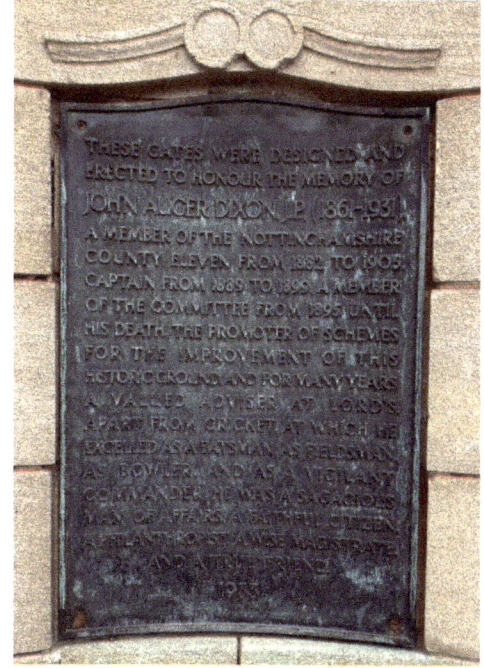

For John, managing a prosperous business meant keeping up with the times, and in the 1916 Wright's Directory of Nottingham, Dixon & Parker Ltd were now listed as tailors, clothiers & motor outfitters. However, John is perhaps most famous for his sporting activities. He played football for Notts. County and was captain of Notts. County Cricket Club. In his memory on the gates at Trent Bridge cricket ground is the featured plaque.

John died on 8 June 1931 after a short illness and left effects of £62,253 3s 9d *(equivalent in 2025 = £5,626,000)*.

The next son, Frederick James, pursued a different vocation and became a surgeon. The 1921 census shows him living with his sister Clara, a social worker, and Frederick working as a medical assessor for the Ministry of Pensions. Both are unmarried.

Incredibly, Frederick lived to the age of 98 and died on 4 March 1863 at St Leonards-on-Sea, Hastings, Sussex. He left effects of £61,388 15s 9d *(equivalent in 2025 = £1,843,000)*.

Now, the youngest son, Charles Percy, became a solicitor. In the 1891 census, he can be found at Haileybury College, Great Amwell, Ware, Hertfordshire, prior to his entering Clare College, Cambridge University, in Michaelmas 1891. He married Louise Robinson in Spilsby, Lincolnshire, on 17 August 1897, and the couple eventually settled at 32 Chestnut Road, Norwood, Surrey. By the 1911 census, Percy, as he was known, was recorded as a *'solicitor but not practising'*, and there may be a reason for that...

Percy was a champion tennis player, and many facts regarding his sporting achievements can be found. In summary, he won an Olympic gold medal in mixed doubles with Mrs Hannan at the 1912 Stockholm Games. Partnering with H. Roper Barrett, they won the Wimbledon Men's Doubles in 1912 and 1913 and were runners-up in 1914. He also reached the Wimbledon singles final twice, in 1901 and 1911.

His other notable wins included the Davis Cup in Australia in 1912 as a player and vice-captain of the Great Britain team, and while he was in Australia, he partnered James Cecil Parke to win the Australian Men's Doubles Title. He had represented Cambridge at rackets, winning the silver medal in 1891. He was also a prize-winning golfer and represented Britain in international fencing in Paris. Quite the sporting chap. Percy died on 29 April 1939, leaving effects of £24,086 7s 8d *(equivalent in 2025 = £2,014,000)*.

And so, the Dixon half of this immensely successful partnership has now been accounted for, but what about Mr Parker?

PERCY DIXON

THOMAS PROSSER PARKER

Thomas was born in Grantham, the son of fishmonger James Astley Parker and Mary Prosser, and his baptism took place at St Wulfram's Church, Grantham, on 18 March 1845. He had two sisters: Anne (1844) and Mary (1846). All seemed well until a search in the 1851 census revealed that six-year-old Thomas and his sisters were recorded living with their grandmother, Gracie Parker, a widow and fishmonger, on the High Street, Grantham. An extensive search of the census records could not locate Thomas's parents, and neither could any death records be confirmed for either of them... All very strange.

In the 1861 census, Thomas, aged 16, was recorded as a draper & outfitter, along with his sister, Mary, now a milliner and living with an aunt named Elizabeth Prosser, who appears to have taken over the fishmongery business on the High Street. She had added poultry to the menu, too.

From here on, Thomas began his meteoric rise to partnership with William Dixon.

Evidently, Thomas was associated with William Dixon in his teens, and at the age of 19, he came to Nottingham and commenced business in a small shop on Lister Gate. Indeed, when he married Mary Ann Baumfield on 15 July 1869 at St Nicholas, Nottingham, his address was recorded as 2

Lister Gate. Hopeful that the marriage record might shed some light on Thomas's father being deceased, it rather confused matters further, as his occupation is recorded as a miner.

Mary Ann's father was hosier Benjamin Baumfield, and interestingly, in the 1869 Morris & Co. Directory of Nottingham, he is listed as a draper, haberdasher and smallware dealer at 4 Lister Gate, next door to Thomas.

Thomas and Mary Ann had eight children, two of whom died young. Minnie Baumfield was the firstborn in 1869, and sadly, she died a year later. Then came Horace Arthur (1870), Lilian Baumfield (1872), Thomas William (1875), Minnie Jane (1876), Ethel Annie (1881) and Grace Vera (1892). Unfortunately, the eighth child has not been identified.

In the 1871 census, Thomas and Mary Ann are recorded living at 33 Pelham Street but then made a permanent move to 3 Elm Bank.

Very little can be found in the newspapers about Thomas, but his partnership with William Dixon was immensely successful. Thomas died on 4 July 1927, aged 82, and left effects of £43,447 19s *(equivalent in 2025 = £3,498,000)*. His wife, Mary Ann, joined him on 21 February 1936, leaving effects of £5919 17s 2d *(equivalent in 2025 = £542,500)*.

Their son, Horace, played a major role in Dixon & Parker, recorded as early as the 1912 Kelly's Directory of Nottingham as a director. He had been educated at the Hoveringham Boys Boarding School, where he was found in the 1881 census. He never married and continued to live at the family home on Elm Bank.

Dixon & Parker eventually closed its doors in 2012, and this concludes the story of its founders.

The button would have been in use between 1864 and the closure of the Grantham Canal in 1929.

THE SITE OF SHOP ON LISTERGATE AS IT APPEARS IN 2025

T Finn & Son – Nottingham
Thomas Finn Snr c. 1774 – 1845
Thomas Finn Jnr 1809 – 1863
John Finn 1811 – 1874
26 Clumber Street/2 Lincoln Street

Of the buttons featured, this one is the oldest in date and can be attributed to Thomas Finn, who was born in Nottingham around 1774. An early mention of him in a newspaper was found on 17 March 1815 in the Nottingham Gazette, when the property in which he was dwelling on Clumber Street was to be sold at auction:

> **BY ELLIOTT & BELL**
> CLUMBER and PELHAM STREET
> TO BE SOLD BY AUCTION
> By Messrs. ELLIOTT and BELL
> *(For the Trustees for Sale on Behalf of Mortgages)*
>
> On Monday the 27th day of March inst. At Three o'clock in the Afternoon, at the Blackmoor's Head Inn, Nottingham, together of in Lots, and subject to such Arrangements and Conditions of Sale as will be then produced:
>
> ALL those TWO Newly-erected Substantial and Handsome FREEHOLD DWELLING HOUSES, with their Outbuildings, yard and Appurtenances, situate in and at the Corner of Clumber Street and Pelham Street, in Nottingham, the most public, valuable and desirable Situation in the Town and now in the tenures or occupations of Thomas Finn and John Mann.
>
> *** For further Particulars apply at the Office of Messrs JAMSON and LEESON, Thurland Hall; or to Mr. STRETTON Surveyor and Architect, Nottingham.
> March 1, 1815.
>
> *(The abbreviation inst. means in the same month)*

He evidently remained in the tenure of the property, as he appears in the 1824 Glover's Directory of Nottingham as a tailor on Clumber Street. In Dearden's 1834 Directory, Thomas is listed at Clumber Street on the corner of Lincoln Street; his brother, David Bennett Finn, is on Long Row. Both were tailors and woollen drapers.

On 5 March 1805, Thomas married Elizabeth Bennett at St Nicholas Church, and they had six children: David Bennett (1806), Mary (1807), and Thomas (1809), who were baptised at the Castle Gate Independent Church. A change of faith saw John (1811) baptised at St Mary's, Arnold, followed by Anne (1813) and Georgiana, baptised at St Mary's, Nottingham.

Now, on 7 July 1830, a theft was reported in the Nottingham Journal:

Perhaps a somewhat severe sentence for the crime committed.

> JOHN LEAPER, aged 14, stole, on the 24th of May, four yards of woollen cloth and half a yard of cotton quilling, the property of Thomas Finn, tailor, his master. – To be imprisoned for nine months.

The Finns are first listed as T Finn & Sons in the 1844 White's Directory, with their house at Forest Cottage. The sons would be Thomas Jnr and John. The listings continued as T Finn & Sons, tailors, drapers & habit makers, until the 1854 Wright's Directory, despite the fact that Thomas Snr had died in 1845. He was buried on 30 May at St Mary's Church, and no probate record can be found for him. Nevertheless, his sons remained in business together until 1857, when it was reported in the London Gazette on 4 December 1857, that the partnership between them trading under the firm of Thomas Finn and Sons was this day dissolved by mutual consent, with the business to be carried on by the said John Finn in the future.

This parting of the ways did not occur before the brothers had carried out good deeds in the community by becoming annual subscribers to the General Hospital for two guineas in 1850 *(equivalent in 2025 = £302.90)*.

Thomas died a bachelor on 25 August 1863, aged 54. Strangely, his probate was not granted until 19 April 1887, by which time the sum of his effects had dwindled to a mere 29s 5d *(equivalent in 2025 = £220.60)*. John continued working at the shop at 26 Clumber Street/2 Lincoln Street until his death on 22 September 1874. He had been living at Park Valley with his sister, Anne, also unmarried. He left effects of under £8,000 *(equivalent in 2025 = £1,002,000)*.

The premises at Clumber Street/Lincoln Street were purchased by Francis Vaughan, the *Thoroughly Practical Tailor, Habit, Breeches & Trouser Maker*.

Five years later, the property was up for sale again, and a description of the building was printed in the Nottingham Journal on 4 January 1879:

> **CLUMBER STREET**
>
> Lot 1. — All that Valuable SHOP with House, extensive Work-rooms, Yard, and Outbuildings in the rear, for many years occupied as a Tailor's Shop, by the late John Finn, and now in the occupation of Mr Francis Vaughan. Also all that Sale Shop in the occupation of Mrs. Band.
>
> This property has a frontage of 28ft. 6ins, to Clumber-street, and of 58ft. 3ins. to Lincoln-street, and comprises an area of 213 square yards or thereabouts. The present rental of the lot is £150 per annum. *(equivalent in 2025 = £20,570.*

At the time of writing in 2025, the building on Clumber Street was on the site of the HSBC bank.

The Finn button would have been in use from about 1844 to 1857.

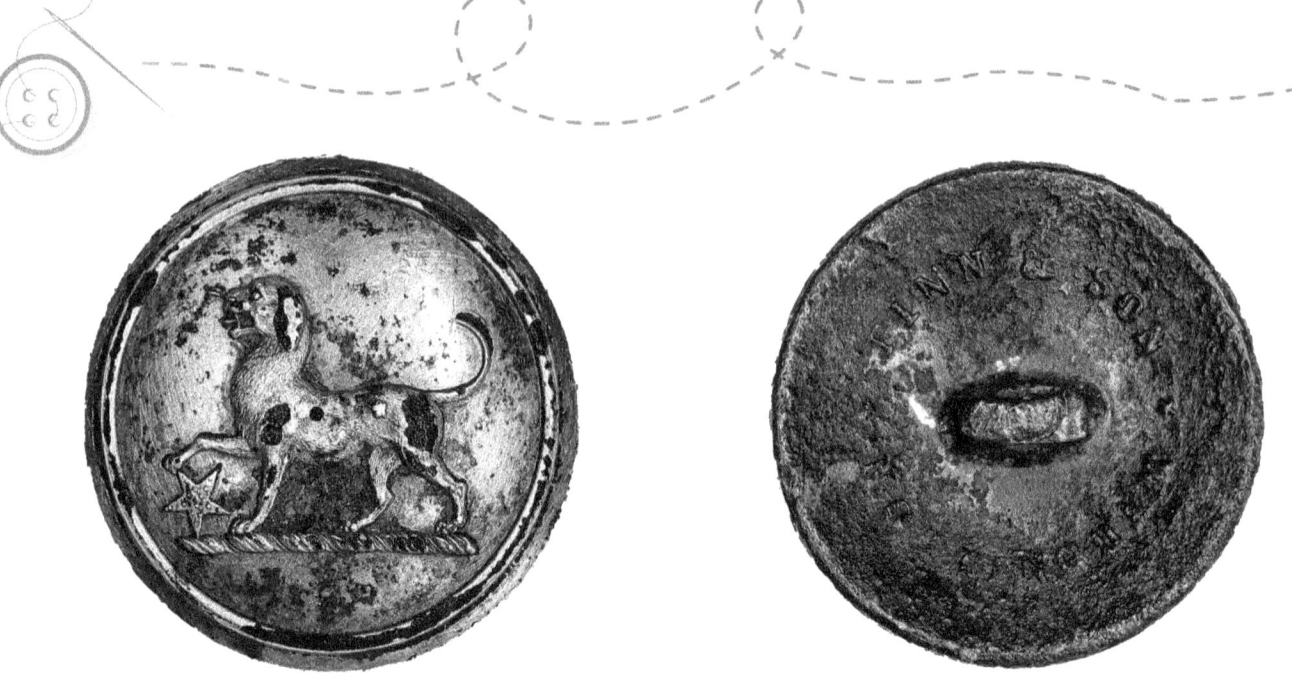

A surprising connection to Finn & Son came in the form of a different type of button, the livery button pictured above. This unusual example bears the name of a tailor, Finn & Son – Nottingham, rather than the maker. There were numerous button manufacturers during the 19th century, but one of the most popular was Firmin in Birmingham or London.

The button shows a Talbot passant (passing or walking by) standing on a rope with its paw on a five-pointed star. In heraldry, a dog symbolises loyalty, faithfulness, reliability, courage and vigilance, while a five-pointed star, also called a mullet, symbolises excellence, nobility and a knight's rank; it is also the mark of cadency for a third son.

Back in the 15th century, the word 'livery' was used to describe the provision of food and keep, which an employer would make available to a servant as payment for services rendered. These liveried servants were issued with badges to wear depicting their master's insignia, and clothing was provided for certain servants, such as footmen. By the 18th century, the heraldic insignia that adorned the servants' clothing was transferred from badges to buttons, and so livery buttons were born. The use of these buttons, to reflect the prestige of an employer's household, peaked in the Edwardian era. Afterwards, there was a steady decline in their use as the gradual momentum of social change was afoot.

When it comes to peers' livery buttons, their status is identified by the respective coronet, such as duke, marquis, earl, viscount or baron, which is placed above the crest.

Finn & Son's button does not feature a coronet, so we can rule out the peers, but it does leave room to consider the possibility that this button was created to showcase the rise and prestige of a new upper class, the industrialists. During the 19th century, Nottingham was well suited on this front, with lacemaking manufacturers taking a prime position. So, did Thomas make servants' uniforms for one of these wealthy Nottingham families and stamp his own mark on the buttons?

W Gabbatiss – Nottingham
William Gabbatiss
1824 – 1904
2 St James's Street, 20 Market Street
&
76 Upper Parliament Street

Walesby, North Nottinghamshire, was the village where William Gabbatiss was baptised on 5 January 1824, the son of labourer Thomas Gabbatiss and Phillis Sansome. Amongst his siblings was his older brother, George, born in 1821.

The family moved around a few of the north Nottinghamshire villages, probably for his father to find work, and in the 1841 census, William was living in Wellow. He was recorded as one of three tailor's apprentices in the household of George Woombell, a tailor. Here William must have learnt his trade, and by the 1861 census he was living at Loverseed Terrace, Nottingham, with his wife Jane Mills, whom he had married in 1858 in Nottingham.

A move to Northumberland Street is noted in the 1864 White's Directory, and by the 1871 census, he was living at 5 Cottage Terrace.
In the 1876 Post Office Directory, William is listed as a tailor at 2 St James's Street. It seemed a popular street to work from, as several buttons in the collection belong to tailors listed there.

Business seemed to flourish steadily over the next few years, and a move to 20 Market Street, a more desirable and prominent street in the town centre, suggests he was doing rather well. This is reflected in the 1881 census, where he was recorded as employing five men. He made a final move to 76 Upper Parliament Street, and in the 1902 Wright's Directory, he is listed as Gabbatiss & Co.; however, it is unknown with whom he was in partnership.

So, other than carrying out a successful tailoring business, what else did William get up to?

Well... he rode tricycles, as did his brother, George, a shoemaker in Newark. Both gentlemen were reported in the newspapers with cycling-related stories.

In the Newark Herald on 16 August 1884, appeared a detailed description of George's *'Long Tricycle Ride'*, a round trip of 100 miles, from Newark to Halifax and back again. *'He asserts that when he completed the distance, he was not in the least degree fatigued or distressed.'*

He was 64 years old at the time.

So, what did William decide to do to celebrate his 72nd birthday? In the Nottingham Evening Post on 19 October 1895:

> Mr Wm Gabbatiss of Nottingham, who is 72 years of age, celebrated his 72nd birthday by riding on his safety bicycle, 72 miles in 11 hours, a great feat for a man of his age. Mr Gabbatiss has ridden for many years, and 19 years ago rode to London on an ordinary in one day.

He placed this advertisement in the Nottingham Guardian on 23 May 1887, perhaps in anticipation of exchanging it for the latest model of tricycle:

> For Sale, Automatic Arkwright Tandem Tricycle: perfect, nearly new; luggage carrier, &c. ; £17 – Mr Gabbatiss, Tailor, Market-street
> *(equivalent in 2025 = £2388)*

William and Jane had no children, and he died, at 8 Dryden Street, on 2 February 1904, at the age of 80, leaving effects of £593 19s 2d *(equivalent in 2025 = £86,310)*. He was buried in Nottingham's Church Cemetery on 5 February 1904. His wife joined him on 2 January 1907, and her effects only amounted to £38 12s *(equivalent in 2025 = £5,507)*.

The timeline for his button ranges from the 1860s to 1904.

19TH CENTURY TRICYCLE

R Goldman – Nottingham
Raphael Goldman
1860 – 1919
19 Carlton Street

Jewish names were often Anglicised, and such was the case with Raphael, who went by the name of Ralph. The first mention of him in Nottingham was found in the Nottingham Evening Post on 8 October 1883:

> IMPORTANT NOTICE. — Ralph Goldman, the Little Champion (late Foreman to Alfred Benjamin) has commenced business for himself as a practical Tailor at 13, Sherwin Street, Mansfield Road. Perfect fit guaranteed as hitherto.

The following year, his advertisement in the Nottingham Evening Post on 5 February 1884 read:

> RALPH GOLDMAN, the Fashionable London Tailor, 19 Carlton Street. Perfect Ladies' and Gentlemen's Clothing.

He certainly meant business, and the shop remained at 19 Carlton Street from hereon.

Ralph was born as Raphael Goldman in 1860, in Spitalfields, London, the son of Abraham Goldman, a Jewish tailor from Russia, and Rachel Raphael from Germany. Ralph married Rachael Cosman Citroen in 1881 in London. She was the daughter of diamond merchant Jacob Cosman Citroen from Amsterdam.

The 1885 Wright's Directory of Nottingham lists Ralph and family living at 13 Sherwin Street. There was a further move by the 1891 census to Leamington Villas, 12 Robin Hoods Close, Nottingham, with their two children, Cosman, who became Maurice (1882), and Annie (1887). Their final move was to 3 Stratford Square, near Shakespeare Street, Nottingham.

The Jewish tailoring community in Nottingham appeared to be close-knit, and an article in The Jewish World on 18 March 1898, illustrates how Ralph and Theobald Alexander the Great (see page 9) must surely have been moving in the same circles – it read:

'*A Purim treat was given to the children attending Hebrew and Religion Classes on Thursday, the 10th inst., at the Central Hall, Shakespeare Street. After a substantial tea, a good programme was gone through, the principal feature of which was a variety entertainment, consisting of songs, sketches and tableaux-vivants, in which Masters Cyril and Victor Alexander and Miss Millicent Alexander (Alexander the Great's children) and a child of four years took part. Ralph, his wife, Rachael and daughter, Annie, contributed to the programmes with many others, and to the Rev. Harris Cohen and Mrs Alexander, who provided all the scenery and stage effects.'*

A further connection between the two men is evident when Ralph took over from Theobald Alexander as president of the Nottingham Hebrew Association, in 1896-98.

However, as in many cases, business does not always run smoothly, as this article in the Nottingham Journal on 23 November 1906 demonstrates:

The final outcome was not reported.

At the outbreak of WWI, many tailors were commissioned to make uniforms, and Ralph, amongst other tailors in Nottingham, became a supplier for the Dayfield Body Shield. These were chest defences produced for private sale by The Whitfield Manufacturing Company of London. Each panel had four steel panels sewn inside the khaki drill covering and sold as *'absolutely bayonet proof'*. They were invented by Francis Dayton and E. A. Whitfield, and the patent was granted on 17 April 1916, for a *'shield that shall be efficient and light and capable of being comfortably worn by a soldier or other person for the protection of his body against attack by rifle fire, bayonet, lance or sword.'*

A LADY'S COSTUME

A lady's green cloth tailor-made costume figured prominently in the Nottingham County Court yesterday, much to the amusement of a large number of both sexes present either on business grounds or out of curiosity.

The plaintiff, Mr Ralph Goldman, costumier, Carlton-street, Nottingham, sued Mr F Holden, The Firs, Halam, Southwell, to recover £7 7s *(equivalent in 2025 = £1,066)*, the value of the costume supplied to the order of the defendant's wife. Mr F Berryman appeared for the plaintiff, Mr F Jackson representing the defendant. The order was executed several months ago, but Mrs Holden, treating the garments as misfits, declined to accept the same. After a critical examination of the articles, and a practical demonstration by Mrs. Holden, who put on the coat and skirt for the purpose, his Honor, by consent, referred the case to a referee for report.

The double version included flexible armoured shoulder straps joining the front and rear panels. They were sold at a price of 21s *(equivalent in 2024 = £96.02)* for the single shield and 52s 6d for the double shield *(equivalent in 2024 = £240.10)*.

(Source: The Royal Armouries Museum, Leeds)

THE DAYFIELD BODY SHIELD

Meanwhile Ralph's son, Cosman, now known as Maurice, was trading as *'Maurice'*, tailor and furrier, on Bridlesmith Gate. Unfortunately, business did not go too well for him. An article in the Nottingham Evening Post on 15 August 1917 tells the story:

FATHER NOT LIABLE FOR SON'S DEBTS.
NOTTINGHAM COUNTY COURT DECISION.

An action was brought in the Nottingham County Court to-day by Mattie Weinberg, the wife of Harry Weinberg, trading as M Cassell, furrier, at Bridlesmith gate, against Ralph Goldman, trading as 'Maurice' tailor and furrier, of Carlton Street, for £10 10s 6d *(equivalent in 2025 = £795.50)* for material and work done between December 2nd, 1914, and January 25th, 1916.

The case of the plaintiff, for whom Mr W B Smith appeared, was that some one named Maurice was trading in Bridlesmith-gate between 1914 and 1916, and he suggested that it was not the defendant, but Goldman's son, Maurice Goldman, gave the orders. Defendant afterwards acquired the business under an assignment, and plaintiff contended that as the goods were supplied in connection with the business, the purchaser was liable.

Mr E Huntsman, for the defendant, stated that the business belonged to, and was carried on by Maurice Goldman, the defendant's son. When the son joined the army he gave to his father a power of attorney to manage the business, but the father, finding the business practically insolvent, instructed Messrs. Mellors, Basden and Mellors to approach the creditors. Ultimately he bought the business for £401 *(equivalent in 2025 = £30,310)* and that was paid to the creditors.

After the parties had given evidence, his honour, being of the opinion that there was no liability on the father, gave judgement for defendant with costs.

Ralph died on 19 February 1919, aged 58, at 350 Mansfield Road, Nottingham, leaving effects of £5478 10s 9d *(equivalent in 2025 = £339,600)*. The executors were Ralph's brothers, Elkin, a tailor, and Jacob, a cap manufacturer.

Following Ralph's death, his shop at 19 Carlton Street continued to be listed in the 1920 Wright's Directory of Nottingham with the abbreviation (exors.). with Mrs Rachael Goldman listed at 350 Mansfield Road. By the 1925 Kelly's Directory of Nottingham, Horne & Harris tailors had taken over at 19 Carlton Street.

Rachael died in London on 6 September 1938 at the age of 79 and is buried in the Willesden United Synagogue Cemetery. No probate record can be found for her.

The timeline for the button would range from about 1883 to about 1920.

Now for Maurice…

As seen earlier, his business sense was not as acute as his father's, and at the time of the court case above, Private Maurice Goldman had joined the Leicestershire Regiment and was suffering hell in the trenches. Alongside the syphilis he had contracted, he caught purulent bronchitis, a deadly respiratory infection that affected British and American soldiers during World War I. It was a distinctive and apparently new infection that occurred in localised outbreaks in 1916-1917. Some scientists and clinicians believe that purulent bronchitis may have been an early manifestation of the Spanish influenza pandemic that followed WWI, killing between 50 and 100 million people.

Maurice was sent back to England unfit for duty and was finally discharged from Carrington Military Hospital on 18 June 1918 with a 20% disability.

Over the next few years, he had his share of ups and downs, but he did continue in the tailoring business. He died in 1943 in Nottingham, and a wonderful tribute to him appeared in the Nottingham Journal on 8 December 1943:

MR. M. GOLDMAN LAID TO REST

Impressive Tribute at Wilford Hill.

Members of the Jewish Ex-Servicemen's Association acted as pallbearers at the funeral yesterday at Wilford Hill Cemetery of Mr Maurice Cosman Goldman, who died at his home, 26, Dryden Street, Nottingham, at the age of 60 last week-end.

A founder-member of the Jewish Athletic Association and the son of one of the founders of the Nottingham Hebrew Synagogue, he was a former holder of the Nottingham billiards championship.

THE SHOP WAS IBERICO IN 2025

W P Groves – Nottingham
William Potter Groves
1856 – 1935
28 Melbourne Street

A Sorrowful Story

William's story starts in Colchester, Essex, where he was baptised on 26 October 1856 at St Giles Church, the son of an Irish tailor and draper named William Benjamin Groves and his wife, Elizabeth Sarah. His father ran a successful business from his home on Newland Street, also known as High Street in Witham, Essex. In the 1861 census, he is recorded as employing three men.

Why William Jnr decided to branch out on his own and move to Nottingham is unknown, but in the 1881 census, he was a boarder at 5 Filey Cottages. Unfortunately, his business was a short-lived enterprise that only ran from 1882 to 1886. During his time in Nottingham, he married Leah Briddon at St Andrews on 1 February 1883. Leah was a local girl, born in 1863, and she had eight sisters. Their parents were George, a bobbin and carriage maker and trimmer, and Maria Smith. They had married in 1845.

William and Leah soon started their family, having eight children together. They lived at 28 Melbourne Street, and that address is where William is listed in the 1885 Wright's Directory. The first five children were born in Nottingham: Beatrice Leah (1883), Maurice Benjamin (1885), Ernest Benjamin (1886), Percy Albert (1887), and Edith Briddon (1889), but their story had a most wretched ending. William is only recorded once in the Nottingham Trade Directories, the reason being that he was declared bankrupt. In the Nottingham Evening Post on 22 December 1886, the *'Failure of a Nottingham Tailor'* was reported.

The failure was set down as having occurred through the debtor over-stocking himself, not having capital to meet accounts, and having given long credit.

William had commenced business in November 1882, his capital being £100 *(equivalent in 2025 = £13,580)*, which he borrowed from Sir Thomas White, and also £320 *(equivalent in 2025 = £43,470)* from his father. Basically, William's outgoings exceeded his incomings, and it was resolved to wind up the estate in bankruptcy.

What happened next?

Between the bankruptcy and the 1891 census, a move was made to Paddington in London, where their sixth child, William Bernard (1890), was born. He died in 1892, and it was a heartache that became the catalyst for Leah's sorrowful story. Our tailor in question was next recorded in the 1891 census, living and working in Stretford, Lancashire, while Leah was at home in Paddington with four of the children. Three-year-old Percy Albert was living with Leah's father in Nottingham.

William obviously returned to his home county, as Leah gave birth to two more sons, Arnold Biscoe (1894 in Finchley, Essex) and Leonard George William (1899 in Braintree, Essex). From here on, some unknown tragedy or illness befell Leah. In the 1901 census, she is recorded as living with her father in Nottingham. William, in the meantime, is on Newland Street in Witham, Essex, having taken over his father's shop. In the 1911 census, William and his youngest sons, Arnold and Leonard, are still at home, but poor Leah has been admitted to Bethnal House for Lunatics. In The Criminal Lunatic Asylum Records, Leah's name first appears in the admissions records on 24 April 1901 and again on 25 April 1906.

She never appears on a census record with her husband or family again.

However, William's is a different story. Having returned to his hometown of Witham, he recovered from his bankruptcy and continued the tailoring business on the High Street. It had been his father's wish in his will that William have the option of taking over his business *'and be recommended, without obligation, that his brother, Alfred, should also be employed in the business.'* William became a successful and well-known man about town, added to which, he was the honorary secretary of the North Essex (Miniature) Rifle Club.

He died in 1935 at the age of 79, and an announcement in the Essex Newsman on 28 December 1935 read:

Of William's sons, Maurice Benjamin followed in the tailoring trade as a cutter and died in 1963. Unfortunately, Ernest cannot be traced after the 1901 census, but Percy Albert became a cabinet maker & wheelwright. He survived WWI, having served in the Army Service Corps and reached the rank of Lance Corporal. His younger brother, Arnold Biscoe, became a tailor's cutter and also survived WWI, joining the Essex Regiment and reaching the rank of 2nd Lieutenant. Leonard George William began his working life as a tailor, but in the 1939 Register he was recorded as a *'farmworker/poultry keeper and a special constable – volunteer duties'*. He died in 1978.

> DEATH OF MR. W. POTTER GROVES. — News has been received in Witham of the death of Mr. William Potter Groves at an advanced age. Mr Groves for a great many years carried on a tailoring business and was one the town's best known personalities. For years he was one of the best shots in the locality. At one time, he was chairman of the Witham Allotment Association, which was but one of his many activities. He was one of the original Witham volunteers. He was also one of the best billiards players and frequently carried off the cup at the Constitutional Club.

William's business in Nottingham lasted only four years, giving us an accurate date for his button ranging from 1882 to 1886.

Leah's story

Leah was admitted to Warley Asylum, Braintree, Essex, on 26 April 1901, when her youngest son, Leonard George William, was only about four months old. Registered as number 15511, she was 37 years old, and her occupation recorded as a tailor's wife. Her record begins by saying that her first attack came on at the age of 27, and she had been 'strange for 10 years, but much worse for the last two months.' This first attack coincided with the birth of her sixth child in 1890, William Bernard, who died in 1892. She was neither epileptic nor suicidal.

On admission, Leah sat talking to herself, occasionally singing and answering questions at random. It was noted that she was dressed, although late in the morning, and her hair dishevelled. She had a wild aspect and threw her lunch about aimlessly. Her physical appearance was noted as '61½ inches tall, weight 100 pounds, eyes dark grey with medium brown hair and her complexion dull and pasty with pimples. Her palate was normal, her tongue straight and clean, but her teeth were decayed.' The record continued by saying that 'Leah was very excited, singing on the day of her admission, yesterday was crying a lot. Today she is more composed but still emotional and began to weep as she talks, she admits to drinking habits and says she has been worried since the birth of her last child a year ago. She has auditory hallucinations or illusions.'

A few days later, on 1 May 1901, acute mania is recorded. 'Leah was very, very excited, singing, shouting, troublesome and could not occupy herself usefully.' This pattern continued over the next months with her hearing voices saying insulting things about her and a repeated comment made by the doctor of 'in good health, but no mental improvement.' Poor Leah was most probably by now institutionalised.

Two years later, on 30 March 1903, there was still no change, and on 20 September the doctor wrote a more detailed report, giving us a glimpse into Leah's fragile state of mind.

'Very industrious and clean, is most evasive in her replies and fences with questions so that I can get very little discreet information, but she refers to hearing insulting voices day and night. Drops hints, "I don't want to be choked so much", but will not explain what she means. One of her remarks led me to ask if she had any propriety, and she replied, "That is best known to my people". Ultimately, she says that her propriety takes the form of, "Homes I suppose, I'm not supposed to know". Her memory is very good and she is in good health.'

Leah's condition never changed. She never returned home and ended her days at Severalls Mental Hospital in Colchester, where she died in 1945 at the age of 81. She had spent more than half of her life in a mental institution, during a time when psychiatric illness was poorly recognised and untreated. Today, Leah could have been diagnosed with postnatal depression, bipolar illness, schizophrenia, or another form of psychosis. That we will never know.

A tragic and all too common story for many women in the 19th and early 20th centuries.

Leah Groves
1863 – 1945

Image of Leah reproduced by courtesy of the Essex Record Office Document A/H 10/2/5/16

Kirk & Son – Nottingham

Joshua Kirk 1828 – 1915
&
Arthur William Kirk
1861 – 1924
23 & 25 Market Street

The firm of Kirk & Son comprised Joshua Kirk and his son, Arthur William Kirk.

The story begins with Joshua…

He was baptised on 9 March 1828 at St Mary's Church, Nottingham, the son of glover and framework knitter George Kirk and Elizabeth. At this time, they lived on York Street. In the 1841 census, George was widowed and lived with his four children: Harriet (1818), George (1827), Joshua (1828) and William (1832). Harriet's occupation is a chevaner, the same as six other women on the same page of the census return. This unusual-sounding occupation was an *'embroiderer on hose'*, one of the additional jobs connected to stocking knitting. George did take a second wife named Sarah. His son, Joshua, was still living at home in the 1851 census, and he was now recorded as a tailor.

Joshua's first listing in the Nottinghamshire Trade Directories was in the 1853 White's Directory at 22 Hockley. On 27 March 1852, at St Stephen's Church, Sneinton, Joshua married Maria Whitehead, who was born in 1834 in Beeston. They had three children: Sarah Elizabeth (1859), Arthur William (1861) and Alice Maria (1869).

Business was growing, and a move of premises took place to 8 Parliament Street. However, as befell many of the tailors in town, Joshua suffered a theft by one of his employees. In the Nottingham Journal, 3 April 1862, it was reported:

> ### THE ROBBERY BY A TAILOR'S APPRENTICE
>
> The youth, John Draper, was brought up on remand, charged with stealing several pieces of cloth, the property of his master, Mr Joshua Kirk, a tailor, Parliament-row. A witness named Oakley, a mechanic of Great Truman-street, spoke in favour of the prisoner's previous character and said he believed his parents were more to blame than himself. The bench sentenced the prisoner to six weeks' hard labour.

A final move to 23 & 25 Market Street took place within the next few years, and an enlargement of his premises was announced in the Nottingham Journal on 13 October 1875:

> ## ALTERATION OF PREMISES.
> # JOSHUA KIRK
> ### TAILOR AND DRAPER, MARKET STREET,
>
> In returning thanks to his friends and patrons for the liberal support accorded him during the many years he has been in business, begs to inform them that for their greater convenience and greater facility in transacting his business,
>
> ### HE HAS CONSIDERABLY ENLARGED HIS PREMISES,
>
> And hopes, by always supplying a thorough, good article at a reasonable price, to merit a continuance of their patronage.
>
> J.K. also begs to inform his friends that he has received large parcels in LATEST NOVELTIES for the approaching AUTUMN SEASON, in SUITINGS, TROUSERINGS, &c.

Joshua would almost certainly have known another of our tailors, Frederick William Beet, whose shop was across the road at 34 Market Street (see page 14).

The Kirk family was now settled at 10 Rookwood Road, St Ann's, and this remained the family home. When Joshua's son, Arthur, came of age in 1883, he became a partner in the business, and henceforward, it became known as Kirk & Son, which is the name featured on the button. However, not all family businesses and relationships run smoothly, as in early 1890, Arthur was in court charged with perjury.

To summarise the case, Kirk & Son had sued Annie Brewin, a woman of somewhat dubious character, for £5 3s *(equivalent in 2025 = £764.40)* for outfits she had made. Her argument for not paying was that Arthur had given them to her as a gift for allowing him to visit her. In court under oath, Arthur denied all knowledge of Annie Brewin being a woman of loose character and denied giving her the outfits free of charge, and that was the perjury committed. Numerous witnesses, all acquaintances of Annie Brewin, gave evidence that they had seen Arthur entering her home on more than one occasion, bringing the outfits for her to try on. Many other witnesses on Arthur's side swore that he did not know the woman, and he had not been in the shop when she came in to order the clothes.

In summing up, the defence told the jury they must look at the class of people called before them. First, a lady who kept disorderly houses, a charwoman or dressmaker employed at the house, a young girl of only 16 years of age living at one of the houses and a man who had recommended Annie Brewin to Kirk & Son as a customer. The judge commented, 'A long experience in this court has taught me this: where women of this character are called, their memories are as frail as their morals.'

Fortunately, the jury was in Arthur's favour, and he was found not guilty.

> *"A long experience in this court has taught me this, where women of this character are called, their memories are as frail as their morals."*

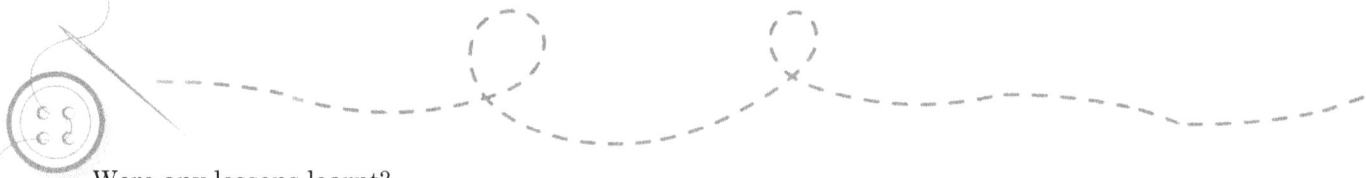

Were any lessons learnt?

On 2 February 1892, the partnership with his father was dissolved, with Arthur continuing the business on his own still under the name of Kirk & Son. Two years later, Arthur was bankrupt. It was reported in the Nottingham Evening Post on 14 March 1894 that Arthur had a salary when he first went into the partnership, and his share in the business was limited to his salary. However, he used to draw out more than his salary if he wanted more. No written agreement was made as to him becoming a partner; the agreement was by 'word of mouth'. There was no record of his father's capital in the business or of the debtor's capital. The partnership was dissolved by mutual consent, with Arthur agreeing to pay his father £1000 *(equivalent in 2025 = £153,600)*. He was to pay £100 *(equivalent in 2025 = £15,360)* down and pay the rest in instalments. He was aware all the time he had been in business that his property was not sufficient to pay his debts in full. Considering that the £900 payable to his father was by weekly instalments of £2 *(equivalent in 2025 = £307.20)*, he thought he had enough profit out of the business to be able to pay the instalments. Sadly, this was not the case, and the receivers were called in.

Arthur was now bankrupt. Although, from the 1900 Kelly's Directory to the 1905 Wright's Directory, either Arthur or his father was trading as J Kirk & Co. Perhaps an investor or two helped Arthur back on his feet again?

Joshua died on 13 October 1915 at the age of 87, leaving effects of £201 17s *(equivalent in 2025 = £21,820)*. Not a huge amount. He was buried on 18 October 1915, and his wife, Maria, died in 1921 at the age of 90.

So, what happened to Arthur?

He had married Alice Mary Bottom on 3 August 1882 at St Thomas Church, Nottingham, but they had no children. After the presumed closure of J Kirk & Co in around 1905, Arthur and Alice made their way down south to Bournemouth, where, by the 1911 census, Arthur had re-established a business and hopefully learnt his lessons.

He died in 1924 at the age of 63, and Alice joined him in 1942, aged 81. Both deaths occurred in Bournemouth.

At the time of writing in 2025, the shop on Market Street would have been located at the site of Belvoir Estate Agents.

The timeline of this particular button would have spanned from 1883 to 1894.

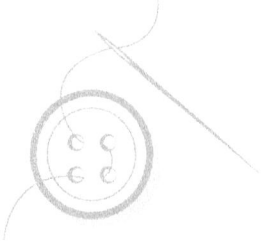

Liverseege – Nottingham

John Liverseege
1792 – 1872

Edwin Francis Liverseege
1822 – 1890

4 Carlton Street, 30 Wheeler Gate & 16 Burton Street

An early advertisement for John Liverseege appeared in the Nottingham and Newark Mercury on 2 May 1829:

> **Summer Fashions**
>
> **J. LIVERSEEGE,**
> TAILOR
> *HABIT-MAKER, AND MAN MERCER,*
> GOOSE-GATE
>
> BEGS leave to return Thanks to his numerous Friends and the Public, for the very liberal encouragement he has been favoured with for the last Seven Years, and hopes by a continuance of his endeavours to give satisfaction, to merit their future patronage and support. He also wishes to inform his Friends in Nottingham and it Vicinity, that he has just returned from LONDON, with a Fashionable Assortment of
>
> **FANCY GOODS,**
> *Adapted to the present Season,*
> Which he has no doubt will give satisfaction to those that will favor him with an early Call.
> Ladies' Habits, Pelisses, Children's Dresses, &c braided and made in the fashionable style.
> Nottingham, May 2, 1829

In Dearden's 1834 History, Directory and Topography of Nottingham, John was listed as a tailor at 4 Carlton Street. In 1846, he also opened a shop in Mansfield Market Place, but this did not seem to be a long-term venture.

So, who were the Liverseege family?

John was born in 1792 in Trowbridge, Wiltshire, and made his way to London, where he married his first wife, Jane Bailey, on 15 May 1817, in Marylebone. The births of two sons are recorded at St Anne's Church, Westminster: John Simon Potter (1818) and Frederick Thomas (1821). Both entries give the address as Queen Street and their father's occupation as a tailor. By 1822, the family had moved to Nottingham, where Edwin Francis was born, and he was followed by Jane Charlotte (1825) and Emma Maria (1828).

John went into partnership with his son, Edwin, in 1844, but two years later, John was widowed when his wife, Jane, died on 24 August 1846 at the age of 64. Nevertheless, a joyful event on New Year's Day 1850 heralded what must surely have been the hope of a fine year when John married for a second time to Sarah Isabella Wood at St Mary's. However, tragedy struck the Liverseege family in August 1850, when it was reported that John's youngest daughter, Emma Maria, died of a short and painful affliction at the age of 22.

Father and son continued to trade from 4 Carlton Street into the 1860s but moved to larger premises adjoining the George Hotel, Carlton Street, in 1865.

Widowed for a second time in 1869, John busied himself with his work until his own death on 19 January 1872 at the age of 80. He left effects of under £800 *(equivalent in 2025 = £96,340)*.

The Liverseege father-and-son partnership of John and Edwin Francis had spanned 28 years.

As for Edwin Francis, he married Catherine Phoebe Bonser (1822), from Kinoulton, the daughter of Samuel and Catherine, on 28 May 1863, in Bunny, Nottinghamshire. They had one son, John Francis (1864), and rather than following in the family tailoring trade, he became a chemist.

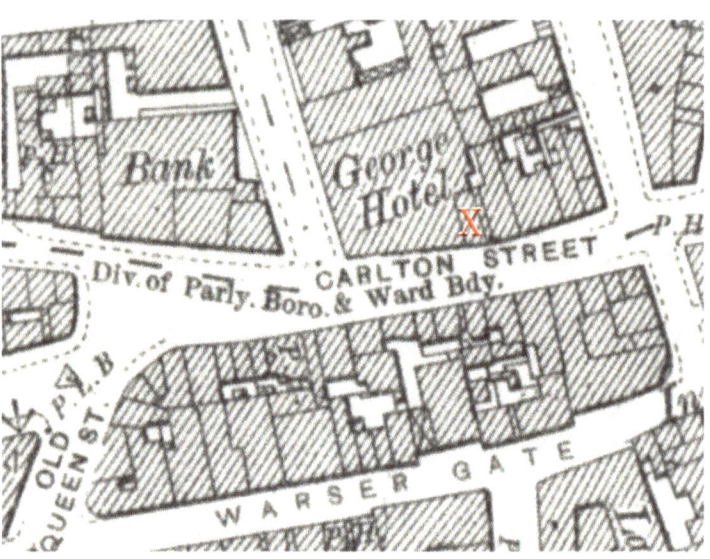

1861 SALMON'S MAP OF NOTTINGHAM
X marking the probable location of the new shop on Carlton Street

After his father's death, Edwin continued to trade as Liverseege & Son. He made a further move of premises to 30 Wheeler Gate, but in the 1888-9 Wright's Directory, he is listed at 16 Burton Street. Edwin died on 14 December 1890 at the age of 68, leaving effects of £714 4s 5d *(equivalent in 2025 = £106,100)*.

Many of the tailors featured were subject to thefts and robberies, and even in his early years, John was no exception, as reported in the Nottingham Review on 22 February 1839:

Despite the captivating description of the coat, it remained unreported whether it was ever recovered from the thief.

The timeline for the Liverseege button ranges from the 1840s to 1890.

> On Friday afternoon last, a black superfine dress coat, having flat buttons, lined at the cuffs with velvet, and bound with silk braid, was stolen from the shop of Mr J Liverseege, tailor, Carlton-street.

Artist – Helen Fergusson

MANDERFIELD – NOTTINGHAM
JAMES MANDERFIELD 1778 – 1871
JAMES JNR MANDERFIELD 1808 – 1888
JONATHAN MANDERFIELD 1816 – 1872
LISTER GATE, ALBERT STREET

The Manderfields were a well-established Nottingham tailoring family throughout the 19th century, situated on Lister Gate and the corner of Albert Street and Hounds Gate. The forerunner was James Manderfield, born in 1778 in East Bridgford, Nottingham. He married Sarah Brittlebank, the daughter of shoemaker Samuel Brittlebank from Heage, Derbyshire, on 20 June 1805 at St Mary's, Nottingham. They had at least seven children, all baptised at the Parliament Street New Connexion Methodist Chapel, formerly Hockley Chapel: James Jnr (26 September 1808 – 1st son), Sarah (about 1811-1844), Miriam (29 April 1814 – 3rd daughter), twins Jonathan and Paul (23 October 1816 – 3rd and 4th sons), and Anna (9 November 1818 – 4th daughter). Unfortunately, baptisms for the other children are missing from the available records. The youngest twin, Paul, died at just over a year old and was buried on 2 August 1818 at St Peter's.

Sadly, their mother was buried on 29 July 1832, at St Peter's, possibly in her late forties, leaving James Snr widowed. He never remarried.

The 1828-9 Pigot's Directory of Nottingham confirms James as a tailor on Lister Gate.

In the Nottingham Review on 6 September 1839, James and two other men were reported as having some unfortunate guttering issues:

> TUESDAY. – Before Mr. Heard and Mr. Gedling
> Informations were exhibited against Thomas Higgins, of Canal-street, James Manderfield, of Lister-gate, and George Dutton, of Glasshouse-street, for not spouting their respective premises, were allowed to stand over for the space of fourteen days.

The men had allowed water to fall from the eaves of the roofs of certain premises in their occupation. Hopefully, the problem was remedied with due haste and the guttering erected.

J. Manderfield, tailor and draper, was advertising in Grace's Guide in 1840, so the spouting incident did not seem to have an adverse effect on business, and a notice in the Nottingham Review on 29 April 1842, informed that James was now in partnership with his son, James, at St Peter's Church Yard and Lister Gate. They continued to trade there for a number of years, with this rather eye-catching advertisement appearing in the newspapers throughout the 1850s:

SEE THE GOODS SOLD AT ALBERT HOUSE ST. PETERS SQUARE

AND JUDGE FOR YOURSELVES

ELEGANCE! EASE!! AND ECONOMY!!!

The astonishing march of intellect in the Arts and Sciences of the present day, has given rise to such active competition, that the Public, and those who desire the combination of Elegance and Economy, have obtained many and great advantages, - and the accurate appreciation of these advantages by the Public is such that their patronage is always conferred just in proportion to the ability to merit it. A strong conviction of this fact has awakened and kept alive an active and persevering determination the mind of J. M., to render to the public every advantage which the progress of modern development can supply; and these advantages will be neither few nor small to those who visit the Establishment of

JAMES MANDERFIELD,
TAILOR, ALBERT HOUSE, ST. PETER'S SQUARE, NOTTINGHAM

Subjoined is a List of Prices:-

Good Fashionable Coats from 18s.; excellent Vests, in great variety, 3s 6d.; good Cloth and Kerseymere Trousers, 12s.; elegant Light Over-Coats, £1 15s.; Children's Cloth Suits, £1; and every description of Clothing really good and cheap,

AT MANDERFIELD'S, ALBERT HOUSE, ST PETER'S-SQUARE.

Drawing of Albert House and St Peter's Square
Artist – Roger Whitehead.

Kerseymere is made from fine wool fibres that are carefully combed and spun to create a smooth, soft texture. The fibres are then woven into a twill pattern, which gives the fabric its distinctive diagonal ribbing. The weave of kerseymere is dense and tight, which helps to make the fabric warm and wind-resistant.

Business flourished, and James Jnr married Ann Spencer on 28 October 1830 at St Peter's Church. They had six children: William (1831), James Frederick (1834), Elizabeth Sarah (1837), Mary Ann (1839), Ellen (1842), and Arthur (1847).

However, sadness befell the Manderfield family over the years. Five of James's children died before the age of 30. William in 1859, aged 28, James Frederick in 1840, aged 6, Elizabeth Sarah in 1858, aged 21, and Arthur in 1866, aged 18, James also lost his wife, Ann, in 1862 aged 53. Disease was rife in all of England's towns but Nottingham had some of the worst slum areas in the country. It was described by the travel writer Celia Fienne at the end of the 17th century thus: *'The town of Nottingham is the neatest town I have seen. It is built of stone and has delicate large and long streets much like London and the houses are lofty and well built. The Market Place is very broad - out of which run two very large streets.'*

Between 1750 and 1830, Nottingham transformed from 'Garden Town' to 'Urban Slum'. The Manderfields were fortunate enough not to be poverty-stricken, but disease shows no mercy and can befall the rich and poor alike.

An almost fatal occurrence was reported in the Nottingham Journal on 23 February 1855:

> On Tuesday a son of Mr Manderfield, tailor, Albert-street, aged 8 years, was sliding near the Trent Company's footbridge, when the ice cracked and he soon disappeared in the water. Another youth, only ten years of age, the son of Mr. Palethorpe, Carrington, being at hand, rescued him at the peril of his own life, and the usual restoratives being applied the lad was taken in safety to his parents.

The young boy in question would have been Arthur, who had an extremely lucky escape, and it is interesting to learn that the canal was still frozen over in February, something that rarely occurs in our present-day climate of mild, wet winters. Arthur may have survived this episode, but he only lived for another 11 years.

In 1846, another alarming incident fell upon James, and it was reported in the Nottinghamshire Guardian on 17 July:

> BURGLARY – At two o'clock on Saturday morning last, Mr James Manderfield, tailor, St. Peter's Church-side, in this town heard a bell ring in his house, whilst he was in bed, and in getting up and going downstairs, he found his shop door had been opened, and was closed again, but not latched. Perceiving several papers had been removed, and hearing a voice in the cellar, he proceeded below, where he found a youth concealed under the cellar grate. On bringing him out handing him over to the Police, he proved to be Charles Betts, a notorious thief; but the alarm had been too early for him, and he had only a few memorandums in his pocket belonging to Mr Manderfield. On searching the young urchin at the watch-house, two sovereigns and four half-crowns were found in his mouth, the produce of another robbery.

By the 1861 census, James Snr was retired and living alone at 16 Pilcher Gate, aged 83. He died in 1871 at the grand old age of 93. He had possibly been living with his son, James, at the time of his death, and no probate record can be found for him.

So, how did James Jnr fare?

He can be found in the 1851 census at Albert House, which is situated on the corner of Albert Street and Houndsgate, recorded as a master tailor employing 18 men. His son, William, was 19 years old and employed as a tailor's shopman, while his younger siblings, Elizabeth, Mary Ann, Ellen and Arthur, were still scholars.

Albert House in 2025

In the 1861 census, the family had moved to Sherwood Place, Sherwood, but they did not stay there long, as the house was *'to be let'* by 1863, with a comprehensive description of the contents for sale appearing in the Nottinghamshire Guardian:

> **SHERWOOD PLACE, NEAR NOTTINGHAM**
> Valuable Drawing Room, Dining Room, and Bed Room FURNITURE, Eight Day's Clock, Chimney and Dressing Glasses, Culinary Utensils, and other Effects. To be SOLD by AUCTION, by Mr. G. HICKLING, upon the premises of Mr James Manderfield, at Sherwood Place. Near Nottingham, on Monday August 10th, 1863, at Eleven o'clock, comprising the Furniture of Drawing Room, consisting of a full Walnut Suite, Dining Room Furniture, Prime Feather Beds, four-post, French and Tent Bedsteads, and Mattrasses, Chimney and Dressing Glasses, Carpets and Druggets, toilet Tables, Wardrobe Dresser, Eight Days' o'Clock, Dolly Wash Tubs, Clothes Horses, Wheelbarrow, Woollen Rugs and other Property. The whole of which will be sold without reserve in consequence of Mr Manderfield having removed to his business premises in Nottingham. The house with large Greenhouse, Garden, &c., to be Let at a moderate Rent.

James Jnr had retired by the 1881 census and was living at Emerson Villa, Mapperley Street, Mapperley. He died on 29 November 1888 at the age of 80, leaving effects of £186 1s *(equivalent in 2025 = £25,970)*.

There is still one more Manderfield to consider as the potential owner of the button, and this is James Snr's younger brother, Jonathan (1816), the older twin. He is recorded in the census as a tailor, employing two apprentices, on Wheeler Gate in 1851 and Middle Hill in 1861. He married Louisa Beard in 1850 at the Brookside Chapel, Derby, with whom he had three children: Sarah (1851), Henry (1853) and Charles (1857).

No large advertisements appear in the newspapers for Jonathan's business. He seemingly tailored away quietly and died on 4 April 1872 at the age of 55, at South Street, Carrington. He left effects of under £450 *(equivalent in 2025 = £50,750)*.

On the contrary, his son, Charles, became a hugely successful lace manufacturer and a senior partner in the firm of Cuckson, Hasledine and Manderfield Ltd. Their warehouse, an impressive Watson Fothergill building, still stands on the corner of Barker Gate and Stoney Street; they also had works on Wollaton Road, Beeston.

In the 1939 Register, Charles' address was recorded as 746 Mansfield Road, and he lived there with his housekeeper, Fanny Campion. There is a separate list of nursing sisters, some of whom have retired, as well as domestic staff living at the same address. A remark in red in the margin reads *'The Convent Nursing Home'*, which is now Woodthorpe Hospital.

Charles remained a bachelor and lived to the age of 94. He died at his home, *'The Elms'*, on the corner of Mansfield Road and Egerton Road, Woodthorpe, on 30 December 1950, leaving effects of £59,210 19s 1d *(equivalent in 2025 = £2,736,000)*. He stipulated in his will that his house should be converted into a nursing home dedicated to his sister Sarah. It was to be named the Sarah Manderfield Nursing and Convalescent Home.

As for the little button, it could be attributed to any of the Manderfield tailors discussed. Perhaps to save money, they just had a batch made up with Manderfield, Nottingham, rather than their individual names. Therefore, the button could have been in circulation from the 1840s to the 1880s.

MATTHEWS & CO – NOTTINGHAM
JAMES WILLIAM MATTHEWS
1851 – 1912
16 ANGEL ROW & 40, 42 & 44 DERBY ROAD

Before becoming Matthews & Co., the business at 16 Angel Row was run by James William Matthews, who worked alone as a hosier, and he is listed as such in the 1881 Kelly's Directory. Two years later, according to the 1883 Wright's Directory, he had taken on a partner or partners and become J. W. Matthews & Co. Around 1905 it became a branch of the well-known Nottingham clothiers and school uniform outfitters, Dixon & Parker (see page 34).

James was born in 1851 in Ruddington, the son of framesmith William Matthews and Mary James. He began his working life as an outfitter's assistant and is recorded as such in the 1871 census, where he was living with his parents and sister, Amelia, on Arkwright Street. Ten years later, he had his own business at 16 Angel Row. Business boomed, and a second branch of Matthews & Co opened at 40, 42, & 44 Derby Road, opposite St Barnabas Cathedral, with displays in the shop windows as advertised in the Evening Post on 8 June 1892:

Money equivalents in 2025:

17s 6d = £128.30
3s 11d = £28.75
15s 6d = £113.70

Was the *'Trent'* hat styled in a particular fashion for Nottingham gentlemen?

Also, this unsolicited testimonial appeared in 1892 from a London customer:

"I can get nothing in Town like your 13s Trousers to measure"

CYCLISTS' SUITS, 17s 6d., at Matthews and Co's, The Clothiers, Derby-road – See Window No. 40.

THE 'Trent' Hat, 3s 11d., is a luxury to wear, the lightest felt hat made; specially manufactured for Matthews and Co., Derby-road; see Window 44A

PARENTS of Little Boys will find a charming variety of Light Tweed, Worsted and Homespun Sailor Suits in delightful shades of drab and grey, from 3s 11d to 15s 6d., at Matthews and Co.'s "The Clothiers" 41, 42, 44 and 44A, Derby-road

PIT Trousers and all Cords and Moles, clearing at greatly reduced prices, at Matthews & Co., Derby Road

By 1899, Matthews & Co. were branching out into football attire, and who could resist a pair of serge football knickers, as advertised in the Football News on 28 January:

(Money equivalents in 2025 range from £11.39 to £34.16)

Added to the shop window displays on Derby Road over the next few years were boys' school uniforms. *'Complete outfits at strictly moderate prices'*. Also, 50s suits *(equivalent in 2025 = £352.10)* to order *'the perfection of tailoring'* and then... in the Hucknall Morning Star and Advertiser on 17 July 1908, *Mother's Darling*:

> FOOTBALL Shirts .
> . . . . . LOWEST QUOTATIONS
> 1,000 PAIRS OF STRONG SERGE FOOTBALL KNICKERS
> 1s 6d, 2s, 2s 6d , 3s 6d. 4s 6d . . . .
>
> MATTHEWS AND Co., DERBY-ROAD NOTTINGHAM

> Mother's Darling
> In a . .
> Matthews' Suit.
> Result: ADMIRING FRIENDS.
>   HAPPY MOTHER.
>
> MATTHEWS & CO., DERBY ROAD NOTTINGHAM

In fact, just about every item of clothing for men, boys, women and girls could be purchased from Matthews & Co.

On 31 July 1876, James married Elizabeth Voce at St Saviour's, Nottingham. By the 1901 census, James and Elizabeth had moved out of the city and taken up residence at 32 Loughborough Road, West Bridgford. The house was renumbered 46 after some of them were destroyed in the WWII Blitz.

James died on 20 October 1912, aged 61. Now retired from business, he left effects of £4455 4s 2d *(equivalent in 2025 = £594,900)*.

It is unknown who James's partners were that made up the '& Co.', but certainly Matthews and Co. continued to trade as a branch of Dixon & Parker and was still advertised as such in 1934.

The button can be dated from 1883 to the closure of the Grantham Canal in 1929.

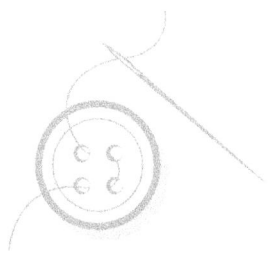

S & J Monk – Nottingham

Samuel Monk
1869 – 1927

James Monk
1872 – 1927

13 Derby Road & 103 Front Street, Arnold

The rather eccentric Monk brothers, Samuel and James, were born in Nottingham to gardener Thomas Monk and Eunice Bates. They married on 29 September 1868 at St Chad, Wilne, Derbyshire, and had nine children: Samuel (1869), Elizabeth (1870), James (1872), Sabra (1874), Amos (1876), Hannah (1878), Mary Annie (1879), Alice (1882), and Lois (1886).

As tailors, Samuel and James are first encountered in the 1891 census at 120 Hucknall Road, Nottingham. The household consisted of the entire family of ten persons, and the brothers are recorded as being employed at this time.

Now, for those not familiar with Mansfield Road, Nottingham, it has quite a slope heading downwards toward the city. Reported in the Nottingham Evening Post on 28 August 1899:

> James Monk, tailor, 20, Hucknall-road, was charged with furiously riding down Mansfield-road on August 9th. P.c. Boot said he was called to Mansfield-road at 2.45 pm on the day in question, but did not see defendant riding. He called two witnesses. – Veterinary-surgeon Taylor deposed that he was driving up Mansfield-road and saw defendant cycling down at a rate of 14 or 15 miles an hour. Some children were crossing the road, and defendant thought he did his best to get out of the way, ran into and knocked down a child aged five. – Similar evidence was given that he was going about eight miles an hour, and that the child in question had almost crossed the road when it suddenly turned back and walked into his wheel. – The bench imposed a fine of 40s., or 14 days in default.
> *Fine equivalent in 2025 = £284.40)*

This escapade did not seem to affect his working life, and by the 1894 White's Directory, Samuel & James had set up a tailoring shop next to the Albert Hall, at 13 Derby Road. They were still listed there in the 1912 Kelly's Directory.

JAMES MONK

James married Mary Ann Hoone in 1899 in Nottingham, and they had four children: John Norman (1901-1986), Decima Eunice (1902), Edna Alice (1903), who died only a few months old, and Vera Muriel (1904).

They first lived at 21 Broad Oak Street and finally settled at 13 Park Place, Park Row. All seemed well until James's wife, Mary, died in 1919, aged 47, and was buried at Lenton Priory on 24 March.

Although James was still recorded in the 1921 census as a working tailor, his death in 1927 told a most pitiful tale:

> ## NOTTINGHAM MASTER TAILOR'S SUDDEN DEATH
>
> ### "TOE-NAILS LIKE LONG HORNS."
>
> **STRANGE NEGLECT**
>
> Remarkable Story at Inquest in Nottingham.
>
> The body was sadly neglected, the toe-nails resembling long horns. The heart weighed 17oz., and I am of the opinion that death was due to failure of the diseased heart.
>
> This was the effect of the postmortem examination report presented by Dr. L. Owen Taylor, at the adjourned inquest on Saturday on James Monk (56) a master tailor of 13, Park-Place, Park-row, Nottingham.
>
> His brother, Amos Monk, of Ratcliffe-on-Soar, said that when he visited his brother last Wednesday the latter complained of a pain across the chest. That night his daughter found him lying dead on the kitchen floor.
>
> Asked by the coroner (Mr. W. S. Rothera) if he could account for the nails being so long, Dr. Taylor said the only reason he could see was neglect. "Only as preserved specimens have I seen such large ones," he added. "They must have gone for years without cutting."
>
> The heart he stated, was twice as large as it should have been.

James was buried on 5 March 1927 at Lenton Priory, and no probate record can be found.

SAMUEL MONK

So, how did Samuel's life turn out? Did he fare any better than his brother?

Prior to the brothers setting up in business together, Samuel placed this advertisement in the Nottingham Evening Post on 25 March 1892:

> TAILORESS. – Wanted, first-class Finisher; £1 5s. per week *(equivalent in 2025 = £171.70)* to a suitable hand will be paid. – Apply Samuel Monk, 10, Clumber-street, over new Hat Shop.

Interestingly, his wife, Zillah Musson, whom he wed on 8 August 1895 at St John the Evangelist, Carrington, was a dressmaker by trade… Had she applied for the job, and did love blossomed over the cutting table?

In reality, their marriage did not appear to be a happy one.

Samuel's shop was situated at 103 Front Street, Arnold, and he just could not keep his name out of the courts and the newspapers. In the Beeston Gazette and Echo on 6 June 1914:

ARNOLD CHARACTER DENOUNCES THE POLICE

WHAT A BIG "B" MEANT

Much amusement was caused at the Nottingham Shire Hall on Wednesday by a case in which Samuel Monk, tailor, of Front Street, Arnold, was charged with using obscene language. P.c. Tomlinson deposed that the offence occurred in the defendant's house at midnight on May 27th, this statement being corroborated by P.c. Hempsall, who said that the language could be heard 20 yards away.

The clerk: have you any questions to ask?

"No, it's a case of one liar supporting another." Replied the defendant, who, when being sworn before giving his version of the affair, exclaimed, " I know all about it; I've been here dozens of times before." He then wrote on paper what he declared he said, and this was handed to the Bench.

The chairman: What does this "B" mean?— That's for supper, sir?

But what does it mean?— "B" for butcher's shop. (Loud laughter).

What Made Him Fierce.

Continuing, the defendant said his wife had got a religious mania, and when he got home she began to talk to him about religion instead of giving him something to eat. The policeman had been living on his door step for the last four months, and it was the fourth time they had had him up at court. "They stand on the door step and glare at me like tigers," cried Samuel waxing still more wrathful. "They are frightened to fight me like men because they know who is the master," he concluded with a thump on the witness box.

The chairman: Don't get excited – I am always likely to get excited when I get sent to prison for 14 days through these dirty vagabonds.

The chairman: You will be fined 20s *(equivalent in 2025 = £115.20)*

The defendant: I refuse to pay on principle.

Only a few weeks before this incident, Samuel had been charged with using obscene language in his shop and for being drunk and disorderly. The police said he was like a wild man.

> *"Police said he was like a wild man"*

Samuel seemed determined to continue causing trouble, as he was back in court less than two weeks later, charged with using obscene language on a train and *'making improper use of the communication cord'*. He was fined another 20s.

Then events turned ugly. Reported in the Nottingham Evening Post on 22 July 1916:

Whether Samuel stopped drinking and calmed down is not known, but Zillah was still living with him in the 1921 census. Samuel enrolled in the Royal Defence Corps during World War I because he was too old to serve on the front lines. The RDC were responsible for guarding important locations such as ports, bridges and railways. For his services, Zillah later received a war pension after his death.

Samuel's demise was now closing in on him…

On 9 January 1926, he collapsed in the street on Mansfield Road, Sherwood, early in the morning and was taken to the Nottingham General Hospital. He recovered from this episode but died on 25 December 1927 at Arnold, aged 58. Despite everything that Zillah had gone through, the death announcement in the newspaper read *'beloved husband of Zillah'*. His interment took place at Redhill Cemetery. He had outlived his brother, James, by only nine months.

Perhaps now that Zillah was free from her husband, she began to live life and was aboard the *SS Majestic* on 3 July 1929, sailing to New York and returning to England in November. The motive for her trip to New York is unknown.

Zillah lived a long life, passing away at Basford Hospital on 11 February 1963, aged 89.

She left effects worth £6710 18s *(equivalent in 2025 = £189,500)*.

As for the little button in this story, the timeline for S & J Monk would be from about 1894 to 1912, using the dates listed in the trade directories.

> **A VIOLENT HUSBAND**
>
> **CASE STOPPED AT THE SHIRE HALL.**
>
> A separation order was made by the magistrates at the Shire Hall, Nottingham, to-day, on the application of Zillah Monk, who summoned her husband, Samuel Monk, a tailor, of Arnold, for persistent cruelty.
>
> Complainant, who was represented by Mr Beck, said that for the last five or six years defendant had been addicted to drink, and his wife had kept him. He had threatened her life, run her out of the house with a stick, thrown the tongs at her, and would have strangled her but for the interference of the neighbours. The house and business belonged to his wife.
>
> The defendant became so violent during the hearing of the case that it had to be stopped for a time. He consulted with his solicitor, Mr W. B. Smith, who, on returning into court, announced that defendant would consent to judgment. Mr Beck said that the woman would be content with a nominal maintenance order, which would be fixed at 4s,. a week. *(equivalent in 2025 = £17.13)*

W T & S Noddall Nottingham & Noddall – Newark

William Thomas Noddall 1813 – 1892
Stephen Noddall 1817 – 1860

14 Stodman Street, Newark, 3 Angel Row, Nottingham & 111 The Strand London

The story of the Noddall button begins in Hull when tailor Stephen Noddall married Elizabeth Dunn on 2 November 1802 at the Holy Trinity Church. Stephen was born in 1781 in Tetney, Lincolnshire, and his father, also Stephen, was the sheriff's officer and an auctioneer. He lived to the grand old age of 90 years.

Stephen and Elizabeth had three children: our two tailors, William Thomas, baptised on 15 October 1813, Stephen on 18 November 1817, and Bennett on 15 July 1815; sadly, he died in 1822. An indiscretion then took place between their father and a woman named Sarah Brewer, resulting in an illegitimate son born in 1821, named Thomas. The death of Stephen's wife, Elizabeth, followed in 1828, and all of these events took place at Great Grimsby, Lincolnshire.

The 1841 census finds the two brothers, William and Stephen, living together in Newark, on Middlegate, and their occupations were recorded as tailors. This fact is supported in the 1844 White's Directory, where they are listed under the heading of Smock Frock Manufacturers and Slop Sellers. Slops were cheap, ready-made clothes. Fast forward to 1850, and in the London Gazette on 30 December, an announcement relating to 111 The Strand reads:

In the meantime, the brothers married and started families.

STEPHEN NODDALL

Although Stephen was the younger brother, it is easier for the timeline to start with him. He married Mary Ann Saltby from Grantham, Lincolnshire, on 24 February 1842 at St Mary's, Newark, and they had five children: Stephen Thomas (1845), Ellen Sophia (1845), John Thomas (1846 – died only a few weeks old), Eliza Gabriel (1847), and Lucy Elizabeth (1848).

Although the London partnership was dissolved in 1850, in the 1851 census, Mary Ann was still living on the Strand with her children and recorded as a hat manufacturer. Stephen, on the other hand, cannot be located. Thankfully, a newspaper report in November 1855 places the family back in Newark. The headline was:

> TAKE notice, that the Partnership for some time carried on between the undersigned, as Hat and Cap Manufacturers, at No. 111, in the Strand, in the county of Middlesex, under the firm of Noddall, Clarkson and Co. hath been dissolved by mutual consent, as from the 25th day of December instant, as regards the undersigned Thomas Charles Clarkson; and it hath been agreed that all debts due to and from the said partnership shall be received and paid by the undersigned William Thomas Noddall and Stephen Noddall. – As witness our hands this 30th day of December 1850.
>
> W. T. Noddall
> Thos. Chas. Clarkeson
> S. Noddall

GRAMMAR SCHOOL DISCIPLINE – EXTRAORDINARY DAMAGES CASE.

To outline the story, the headmaster of Newark Grammar School sued Stephen Noddall for damages caused to a door in the school. It transpired that Stephen had requested that his son, Stephen Thomas, take a day off school, which the headmaster refused, but Stephen kept his son off school anyway. Because of this, Stephen Thomas was punished for his father's wrongdoing and put in after-school detention for two weeks alongside numerous other boys. Stephen was furious and entered the school determined to rescue his son from the tyrannical headmaster, resulting in him damaging the door lock of the room in which the boys were being kept. Much unpleasantness was passed on either side in court, but the jury ruled in the headmaster's favour, and Stephen was ordered to pay damages of one shilling and nine pence *(equivalent in 2025 = £11.09)*, the amount of damage done to the door lock.

The court case would no doubt have cost much more than that.

Stephen and Mary Ann were only married for 18 years, as Stephen died in 1860, aged 43, and was buried on 8 May at St Mary's, Newark. For some reason, his probate was not granted until 27 September 1878; his effects were under £1500 *(equivalent in 2025 = £196,400)*. Following Stephen's death, his wife continued running the business on Stodman Street, but further sadness struck the family when their son, Stephen Thomas, died on 25 November 1871 at only 28 years of age.

In the 1881 census, Mary Ann, now aged 70, had moved to 54 Humberstone Road, Leicester, and was running a fancy goods business. Her two daughters, Ellen and Eliza, were with her, together with Mary's sister-in-law, Mary Clarkson. Mary Ann died in 1886 at the age of 75, but no probate record can be found for her.

Now, back to William.

William Noddall

William Thomas married Elizabeth Aldridge on 23 September 1841 at Rolleston, Nottinghamshire, and they had two daughters: Mary Ann (1842) and Lucy Elizabeth (1848). Their marriage lasted only eight years, as sadly, Elizabeth died in 1849 at only 37 years of age, just a few weeks after giving birth to Lucy. She is buried at St Mary's, Newark.

The 1851 census records William, with his daughter, Mary Ann, a housekeeper and a servant living at 14 Stodman Street, Newark, and his occupation as a master tailor, employing 25 men and 30 women. His other daughter, Lucy Elizabeth, was living in Rolleston with her grandfather, John Aldridge, a farmer.

Although no marriage record can be found, William took a second 'wife', Ann, born in 1822, in Wood Newton, Northamptonshire.

Alongside the Newark shop, William and Stephen ran one in Nottingham, at 3 Angel Row, also known as Market Place, and this advertisement appeared in the Newark Advertiser on 13 July 1859:

> **NOTTINGHAM AND NEWARK**
> MIDLAND COUNTIES TAILORING ESTABLISHMENTS.
> W. T. AND S. NODDALL
> STODMAN STREET, NEWARK,
> AND MARKET PLACE, NOTTINGHAM
> THEIR SUMMER STOCK NOW READY

> **GENLEMEN'S WINTER CLOTHING,**
> OVERCOATS, &c.
> **NODDALL & CO.,**
> 3, ANGEL ROW, NOTTINGHAM,
> and Stodman-street, Newark
> TAILORS AND WOOLLEN DRAPERS,
> Invite attention to their Large and Varied Stock of material for
> **WINTER CLOTHING**
> of every description, and assure their customers of obtaining good value, good style, and good fit.

Spot the misprint in this later advertisement in the Nottingham Journal on 4 January 1872:

By September 1873, Wm Gibbons Wilson was advertising that he had taken over the Fashionable Tailoring Establishment of Messrs. Noddall & Co at 3, Angel Row (see page 81).

Why William sold this part of the business is unknown. At the time he was living on Park Valley, Standard Hill, a stylish area of Nottingham, and recorded in the 1871 census as a tailor and draper employing 45 hands. However, he returned to Stodman Street, Newark, perhaps taking over from Stephen's widow and scaling down the business somewhat to employ nine men and one boy by the 1881 census. By the 1891 census, William was widowed again, but he continued to work until his own death on 25 September 1892 at the age of 79. He was buried on 28 September at Newark Cemetery in an unpurchased grave, Section E1, number 122, with his wife, Ann, who was buried on 7 March 1886. As it is a common grave, interred between them is a ten-year-old girl named Lily Aldridge, who was unknown to the Noddall family.

The timeline for the W T & S Noddall, Nottingham button would have to be from the 1850s to about 1860, when Stephen died, and the Noddall – Newark button, anytime from the start of their business to William's death in 1892.

Artist – Julie Penaluna

Porter & Co – Nottingham
Gregory Porter 1829 – 1889
William Christopher Porter 1857 – 1932
Henry Ogle 1862 – 1917
4 Parliament Street & 19 Clumber Street

The Sewing Schoolmaster from Southery

This button tells the rather unusual story of a schoolmaster who was also a senior partner in a tailoring business.

Gregory Porter was baptised on 8 March 1829 at Southery, Norfolk, the son of William and Elizabeth. Gregory's first occupation was a cabinet maker, which is recorded in the 1851 census when he was a visitor in the household of William Casebow, another cabinet maker. Gregory then made a move to Nottingham and reinvented himself as a schoolmaster.

He married Elizabeth Moreton Shipman in 1859 in Nottingham and opened his first school on Annesley Grove just prior to this. The school is listed in the 1858 Wright's Directory of Nottingham as a day school. He soon moved to new premises at Cleveland House, Mansfield Road, not far away, as advertised in the Nottingham Journal on 21 January 1859:

A final move to Tudor House, 10 Balmoral Road, was made later. In the 1871 census, Gregory had 17 boys boarding at the school, an assistant master called William Tugwell, and his wife, Elizabeth, was the school headmistress.

> CLEVELAND HOUSE, MANSFIELD ROAD, NOTTINGHAM (late Annesley Grove) – BOARDING and DAY SCHOOL for BOYS. – Mr. GREGORY PORTER begs to inform his friends and the public generally that the duties of his School will be resumed on Tuesday, January 25th, 1859 – Prospectus with references forwarded on application.
> Cleveland House, Jan. 11th, 1859.

Gregory and Elizabeth had two sons: Gregory Alfred (1859), who died at the age of 14 in 1874, and Frank Constable (1869), who became a wealthy and presumably successful dental surgeon, as evidenced by the £76,529 7s 11d *(equivalent in 2025 = £3,242,000)* estate he left in 1951.

Sadly, Gregory's wife died in 1874, in Derby, at the age of 34, and her death occurred within the same registration quarter as her son, Gregory; how tragic for Gregory Snr. However, he married a second time to a widow, Mary Hudson née Padley, on 20 April 1878, in York. The name Padley will feature later… So, how did Gregory become involved in a tailoring firm?

Gregory had retired from the school by the 1881 census, and at about this time, his 23-year-old nephew, William Christopher Porter, arrived in Nottingham. In the same census, he was recorded as a tailor & habit maker, and in the 1881 Kelly's Directory, Porter & Co. are listed as tailors and habit makers at 4 Parliament Row, later moving to 19 Clumber Street. Presumably, Gregory and his nephew were now in partnership.

William Christopher was born in 1857 in Southery, the son of Gregory's brother, William Christopher Porter, and his wife, Martha Brown. William Jnr married Laura Elizabeth Butler, the daughter of Nottingham hosier Haywood Butler, on 3 November 1886 at Carrington Church.

The partnership between Gregory and William did not last long. It was announced in the London Gazette on 11 August 1888 that it was to be dissolved, with Gregory continuing the business under the present style or firm of Porter & Co.

Now, Gregory was not a tailor, so who was his next partner?

In the 1881 census, an 18-year-old tailor's trimmer named Henry Ogle lived at 36 Lincoln Street, on the corner of Clumber Street. He may already have been employed by Gregory, but Henry certainly became his partner. Henry was born in Hucknall Torkard in 1862, the son of malster John Ogle and Eliza Williamson.

Once again, this partnership was short-lived, not by mutual consent but by Gregory's untimely death. He died on 29 August 1889 at the age of 60, and it was reported in the Nottingham Evening News on 30 August 1889:

THE SUDDEN DEATH OF A NOTTINGHAM TRADESMAN

The Deputy Borough Coroner (Mr. A. Browne) held an inquest this afternoon at the Lion Hotel, Clumber-street, on the body of Mr. Gregory Porter of 10, Burford-road, who suddenly expired at his place of business, 19, Clumber-street, on the previous day. The deceased, who was 60 years of age, was the senior partner in the firm of Messrs. Porter and Co. – Mr George Padley, of Scarborough, deposed that the deceased was his brother-in-law. The last time he saw him alive was about three weeks ago, when he was on a visit to Scarborough. He was in feeble health when he arrived, but when he left, he appeared to be somewhat better. John Ogle, of 7, Oliver Terrace, Portland-road, salesman, lately in the employ of the deceased, said that on Thursday morning Mr Porter came to business as usual. At about half-past eleven the deceased came down stairs from his private room, and a quarter of an hour afterwards witness went up to him and they talked about the strike in the lace trade in Nottingham. On going up again to the deceased's room, at half-past one witness found him leaning back in his chair. He saw at once that Mr Porter was dead. There was an unfinished letter lying on the table. – Mr C. Haydon White, surgeon, said he had attended the deceased for the last five years. He suffered from sluggishness of the liver and a feeble heart. He ascribed death to heart disease. – The jury returned a verdict in accordance with medical evidence.

Poor Gregory. He left effects of £4378 14s 7d *(equivalent in 2025 = £652,800)*.

The story is not yet over, though. After Gregory and his nephew parted company, William and his wife, Laura, emigrated to the USA, and in the 1900 Federal Census of America, they are recorded living in Manhattan with William employed as a clothing cutter. Their date of immigration was 1889, the same year that Gregory passed away. Unfortunately, Laura died on 6 March 1904 in Manhattan, and her death made it into the Nottingham Evening Post three days later:

> PORTER. – ON THE 6TH INST., AT New York, Laura Elizabeth, the dearly loved wife of William C. Porter, and youngest daughter of the late Haywood Butler.

Not all was lost for William, for he married again to Ada, a hairdresser from Connecticut, 27 years younger than himself. Their names appear on a passenger manifest in 1928, sailing from Cherbourg, France, to Southampton and then to Quebec. They were in Manhattan in the 1930 Federal Census, when William was 73 and still working as a tailor.

He died in there on 15 February 1932 – quite a journey from sleepy Southey to manic Manhattan!

Porter & Co. carried on trading successfully under the management of Henry Ogle, and he moved the shop to 47 Clumber Street. Porter & Co. continued to trade following Henry's death in 1917, making a move to 9 Clinton Street during the 1940s. The last entry in the British Phone Book for Porter & Co. was in 1953. That is some longevity for a business started by a retired schoolmaster and his nephew in 1881.

Our Porter & Co. button would have been in use between 1881 and 1929 at the closure of the Grantham Canal.

LUSH WAS THE OCCUPANT OF 19 CLUMBER STREET IN 2025

T Sharp – Nottingham
Thomas Sharp
1818 – 1907
St James's Street, High Street,
10 Victoria Street & 4 Thurland Street

With eight Thomas Sharp buttons in the collection, you might be forgiven for thinking he needed to sew his buttons on more securely, or perhaps he was a very successful tailor and outfitter.

Thomas was baptised on 25 February 1818 at St Peter's, Nottingham, the son of tailor John Sharp and Elizabeth. He had numerous siblings: John (1814), Mary (1816), Henry William (1822 – died at 7 months), Henry (1822), Elizabeth (1824) and Selina Ann (1826). The Sharp family first lived on Wheelergate and then on Low Pavement.

His first shop was on St James's Street in Nottingham, a popular street for tailors (see William Gabbatiss page 50), and Thomas is recorded in the 1841 census living on Long Row West, possibly at the junction with St James's Street.

Thomas married Elizabeth Talbott, the daughter of victualler Francis Talbot, on 28 December 1839, at St Matthew's. Their son, Francis Talbott Sharp, was baptised on 5 May 1840, at St Mary's. Unfortunately, Elizabeth died a few years later and was buried at St Peter's on 4 April 1848, aged 35.

In terms of his working life, as early as 1845, Thomas placed a notice in the Nottingham and Newark Mercury informing of his return from London with his newly selected stock. His business thrived, and a move to High Street placed him nicely situated in the centre of Nottingham.

Then, on 30 April 1852, in the Nottingham and Newark Mercury, he placed a rather grand advertisement embellished with a royal crest:

WOOLLEN DRAPERY AND TAILORING ESTABLISHMENT,

HIGH STREET
NOTTINGHAM APRIL

THOMAS SHARP

Respectfully announces his return from London. His Stock is now replete with the choicest and most Fashionable Styles of GOODS for the approaching Season.

Those who appreciate a genuine good article at the lowest possible cost, and who PROPERLY ESTIMATE ULTIMATE SATISFACTION, TRUE ECONOMY, and PUNCTUALITY, may secure such results at this Establishment.

Thomas was making a good enough living to send his son to boarding school, and ten-year-old Francis can be found in the 1851 census at Auburn House, Narborough, Leicester, a boarding academy run by George Wills. This education served him well as he became a veterinary surgeon at the Royal Veterinary College, London. His occupation was recorded thus in the 1861 census, when he was living with his father at Elm Avenue.

Profits also allowed Thomas to provide a day out for his workers. It was reported in the Nottinghamshire Guardian on 11 August 1865:

The average number of his employees between the 1861 and 1881 censuses was about twenty-five. In 1871, he also employed one woman – was she allowed on the Away Day?

A further change of business premises took place at Easter 1866, to 10 Victoria Street, Nottingham, next door to the Daily Express Office; this office later relocated to Upper Parliament Street. At the request of many customers, Thomas now intended to add a new Gentlemen's Outfitting Department.

> TREAT TO WORKMEN.— The workmen in the employ of Mr. Thomas Sharp, tailor, High Street Place, had their annual treat on Monday, the 7th inst., at the house of Mr. Cupid, Stoke Ferry, when they were entertained to a substantial breakfast, dinner and supper. After the cloth was drawn, the health of the employer was drunk, and heartily responded to. The remainder of the evening was spent in songs, recitals, &c., when the party returned home, highly gratified by their day's enjoyment.

Interestingly, Francis, the veterinary surgeon, gave up this career to join his father. He described himself as *a veterinary surgeon, no longer practising, now a gentleman's outfitter* in the 1881 census.

Thomas had married a second time on 26 July 1861 at St Matthew's to Eleanor Winter, a schoolteacher born in 1828, the daughter of architect Thomas Winter. Intriguingly, Eleanor's much younger sister, Caroline (1843), married Francis (the vet) on 20 July 1875, also at St Matthew's. By 1891, both families had moved out of Nottingham to Radcliffe-on-Trent and were living on Shelford Road, close to the railway station. A most convenient location for commuting into Nottingham. A further change of business premises to 4 Thurland Street was listed in the 1902 Wright's Directory.

Sadly, Eleanor died in 1895 at the age of 66, and Thomas joined her on 22 August 1907, aged 89, leaving effects of £30,878 18s 3d *(equivalent in 2025 = £4,406,000)*. Only three years later, Francis died on 11 November 1910 at the age of 70. He left effects of £20,858 5s 4d *(equivalent in 2025 = £2,872,000)*.

The remaining Sharp family, Francis's widow, Caroline, and her two daughters, Lucy and Daisy, continued to live at their home in Radcliffe-on-Trent, which in the 1921 census is recorded as Campbell House. Lucy and Daisy were unmarried, and both of them served as nurses in World War I.

The eight lost buttons, labelled 'T Sharp', 'Thomas Sharp' and 'T Sharpe', would have found their way into the Nottingham night soil between about 1840 and 1910.

W W Sibley – Nottingham
W Sibley – Nottingham
W Sibley Junr. – Nottingham

William Wicher Sibley
1807 – 1885
William Wicher Sibley
1835 – 1915
William Wickham Sibley
1865 – 1947
1 Pelham Street & 12 Clumber Street

The two buttons feature W W Sibley (William Wicher Snr and Jnr) and W Sibley Jnr (William Wicher Jnr)

William Wicher Sibley Snr came from London, and his initial occupation, recorded in the 1841 census in Nottingham, was a pawnbroker at 1 Pelham Street. However, he is listed as a tailor and clothier in the 1844 White's Directory of Nottingham.

He was baptised on 12 August 1807 at St Marylebone, London, the son of schoolmaster George Sibley and Christian Baker. William made his way to Nottingham and married Hannah Wickham at St Mary's on 18 August 1830. They had three children: Jane Baker, baptised on 7 March 1832, Hannah on 19 November 1833, and William Wicher (Jnr) on 25 November 1835. At each of these baptisms William is recorded as a pawnbroker.

In 1838, when the children were very young, Hannah died at the age of 34 and was buried at St Mary's on 18 August. However, William married for a second time to Ann Eliza Cartwright in Loughborough on 14 April 1841. Ann was a minor when they married, and the marriage licence states that she was *'of the age of eighteen and upwards, but under the age of twenty-one years'* and a spinster. Her father was Daniel Cartwright, a bookseller, and he made an oath that he had granted his consent for the marriage.

William and Ann Eliza had eight children: Oliver Cartwright (1844), Daniel (1845), George (1848), Anna Eliza (1853), Henry Edward (1855), Harriet (1858), Thomas Alfred (1860) and Walter Whicker (1862). Reading through the baptism records, William's occupation changed from pawnbroker to tailor at Daniel's baptism.

Then, a most interesting entry in the 1862 Wright's Directory of Nottingham came to light. William Wicher Snr was a committee member of the Anacreontic Society, a popular gentlemen's club of amateur musicians founded in the mid-18th century, initially in London. The London Society came to an end in about 1792 when the Duchess of Devonshire attended a meeting, and as some of the comic songs were considered a little bawdy for ladies, the singers were restrained. The disgruntled singers began to resign, and eventually the society was dissolved.

This did not prevent the society from continuing in numerous other towns in England, and it was extremely popular in Ireland. Indeed, in Nottingham, where William was a member, they met at the Crown and Cushion Inn, which was situated on modern-day Weekday Cross, formerly known as Mont Hall Gate, Blowbadder Street and Market Street.

In the Nottingham and Newark Mercury on 27 October 1843, there was a notice as an encouragement to native talent. The Committee proposed awarding Premiums for two Glees to be produced for 26 January 1844.

Furthermore, in different newspapers in 1855, the Nottingham society was advertising a prize of five guineas for the best glee, male voices, subject *'The War'*. The competitors had to be natives or residents of Nottinghamshire. *(Equivalent of 5 guineas in 2025 = £602.00).*

The most surprising feature of the society was their song. Written in the 1780s by a Gloucester man named John Stafford Smith, it became popular in England and America and eventually became the tune for The Star-Spangled Banner.

Now back to William.

Also in 1855, like many of our tailors, he had a pair of trousers stolen from outside his shop. At the trial, even though the thief was imprisoned for two months with hard labour, the judge passed comment that he often expressed his strong disapprobation of the practice of exposing goods for sale outside the shop.

> *"Often expressed his strong disapprobation of the practice of exposing goods for sale outside the shop."*

William's wife, Ann Eliza, died on 1 December 1865 at the age of 43. Widowed for a second time, he was again left with their children to raise, the youngest of whom was just three years old. Nevertheless, his eldest son, William Wicher Jnr, had already joined his father at the shop, although in the 1871 census, they were both found in Worthing, Sussex. Perhaps they were on a business trip or enjoying a refreshing seaside break? Regardless, they soon returned to Nottingham.

William Snr died aged 77, on 10 January 1885. The inquest into his death was reported in the Nottingham Evening Post three days later:

> FATAL FALL IN NOTTINGHAM. — The Deputy Borough Coroner, Mr A. Browne, held an inquest last evening at the Craven Arms Inn, Woodborough-road, touching the death of William Whicher Sibley, aged 77 years.- Mr. John Thomas Whitehorn, auctioneer, of 41, Shakespeare-street, stated that the deceased was his father-in-law. Deceased had formerly been a pawnbroker and clothier, but had recently retired. He had been in failing health for some time past. Witness saw deceased on Friday afternoon, the 2nd inst., when had a fall. He had a bruise on his forehead and was in a half conscious state. Witness remained with him till he became quite conscious, and he then told witness that he had been out for a walk when he slipped and fell. Deceased was brought home by two young ladies. He was capable of walking about and taking care of himself. Deceased died on Saturday. — Sarah Jane Dove, of Bangor-street, deposed to seeing deceased on Friday, the 2nd of January, on Peas Hill-road. He lay on the ground, and witness helped pick him up. Witness and her sister helped him along for some distance, and he then asked for a cab. Witness found out where he lived, and he was taken to his home at 280, Alfred-street. Deceased said he had caught his stick against a doorstep, and fallen down,- Mr C V. Taylor, M.D., stated that he was first called in to see the deceased on the evening of January 2nd. Deceased was in a semi-conscious condition, and was suffering from a contusion in the centre of the forehead, a small lacerated wound on the bridge of his nose, a contusion on the left cheek, and his left wrist was sprained, Witness attended deceased up to the time of his death. The cause of death was climacteric decay, combined with the effects of the fall.— The jury found a verdict in accordance with the evidence.

He left effects of £831 11s 6d *(equivalent in 2025 = £121,100).*

When William Wicher Jnr took over the business, he moved to 12 Clumber Street. He married Isabella Alvey, the daughter of rag merchant William Alvey, on 22 April 1862 at St Mary's. They had three children, but theirs was a sad story. The firstborn was Isabella in 1862, but she died only a few weeks old and was buried on 20 November 1862. William Whicker Sibley, born in 1865, fared much better and survived childhood and beyond; however, his younger sister, Amy, sadly suffered the same fate as Isabella and also died only a few weeks old. She was buried on 17 September 1870.

By 1900, William Jnr and his son, William Whicker, were listed in Kelly's Directory as William Sibley & Son, tailors, at 12 Clumber Street. The last listing for William Sibley & Son was found in the 1914 Wright's Directory, as William Jnr died on 1 November 1915, aged 80. His effects only amounted to £12 10s *(equivalent in 2025 = £1,351)*.

His son, William Whicker, did not continue the business. He was recorded in the 1921 census as a commercial traveller, living at 185, Rolleston Drive, Lenton. He had married Edith Florence Rogers, the daughter of chartered accountant Charles Rogers, on 1 February 1894 at St Andrew's. Their children were Claude (1894), Florence Isabell (1896) and Harold William (1898). Interestingly, Florence, who later added Eileen as a first name, married Charles Edward Mooney in Montreal, Canada, on 20 September 1922.

William Whicker died in 1947 at the age of 80, and no probate record can be found for him.

The timeline for these buttons ranges from 1848 to 1915.

THE BRITISH HEART FOUNDATION WAS THE OCCUPANT OF 12 CLUMBER STREET IN 2025

Wilson & Son – Nottingham
W G Wilson – Nottingham
Wilson – Angel Row

Joseph Wilson c. 1824 – 1893
William Gibbons Wilson 1844 – 1876
Henry Joseph Wilson 1848 – 1893
Goose Gate & Angel Row

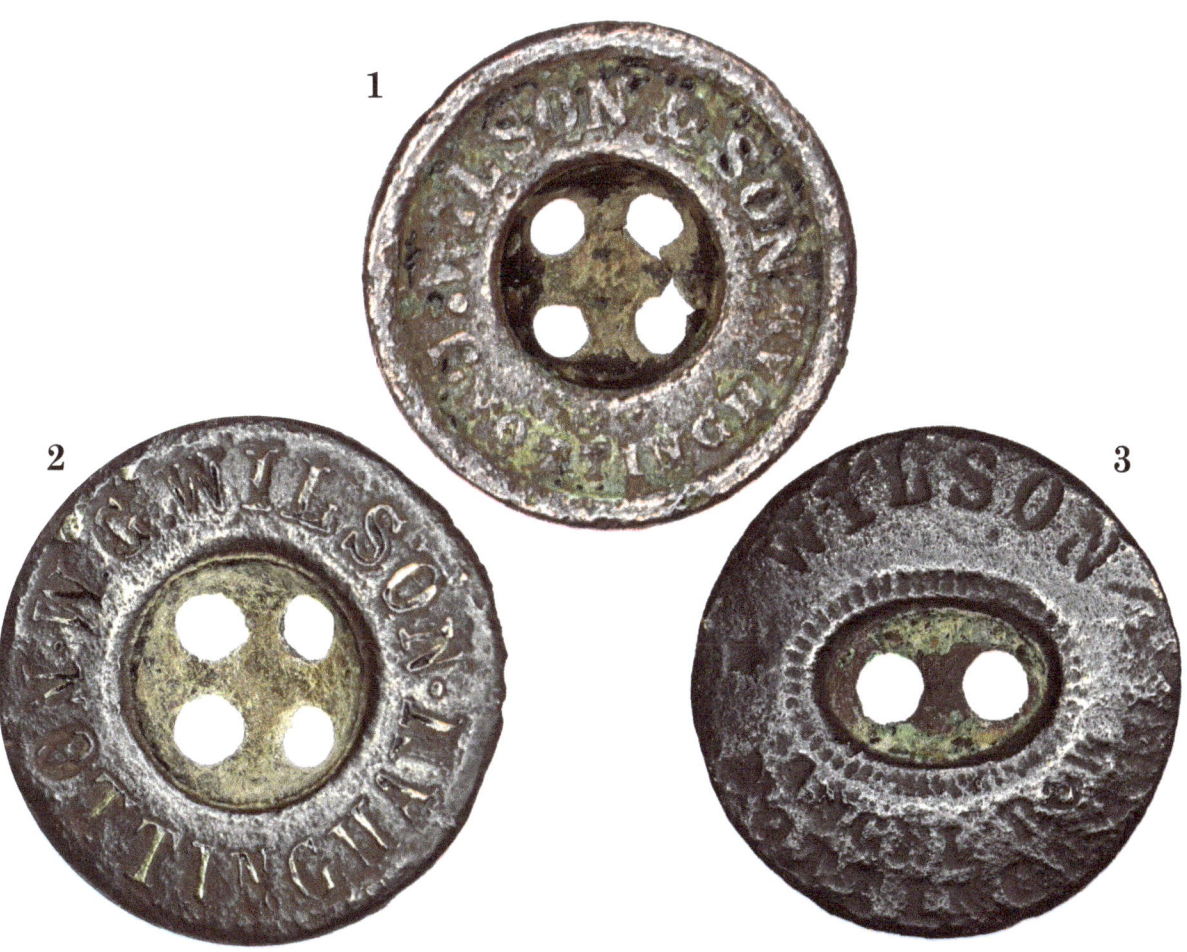

Three buttons connected to the Wilsons are among the collection: 1. Wilson & Son – Nottingham, 2. W G Wilson – Nottingham, and 3. Wilson – Angel Row, and each button is linked to different members of the same family.

Button 1 – Wilson and Son – can be attributed to Joseph Wilson and one of his sons, at the shop on Goose Gate, Nottingham.

This advertisement appeared in the Nottingham Journal on 3 February 1866:

Following the Great Exhibition at Crystal Palace in 1851, other towns in England caught the exhibition fever and decided to host their own, including Nottingham. It was opened on 12 September 1865 by the Right Honourable Lord Belper and named the Nottingham and Midland Counties Working Class Art and Industrial Exhibition. A magnificent building was erected on Horse Fair Close to house the exhibition, which ran parallel to Shakespeare Street.

Joseph Wilson certainly cashed in on the act with the suit he displayed at the fountain, which could have looked similar to the featured illustration.

> **J. WILSON AND SON**
> PRACTICAL
> *TAILORS, WOOLLEN DRAPERS, AND HATTERS,*
> 22, GOOSE-GATE, NOTTINGHAM,
> BEG TO CALL THE ATTENTION OF VISITORS TO THE
> *INDUSTRIAL EXHIBITION*
> To their BRAIDED KNICKERBOCKER SUIT, now exhibited on an elegant Wax Figure, near the Fountain.
>
> EXHIBITION SUITS............£3 10 0
> EXHIBITION TROUSERS.........16 6
>
> Great variety of FASHIONABLE OVERCOATS, including the new PRINCE ARTHUR JACKET.
> Prices from £1 1s to £3 3s
>
> Orders of every Description Promptly executed.

Artist – Helen Fergusson

Joseph was born in Nottingham in about 1824, and by the 1851 census, he had already established himself as a tailor employing four men at his home and premises on Goose Gate, Nottingham. Living with him was his wife, Edna née Gibbons, whom he had married in 1844, and their two sons: William Gibbons (1844) and Henry Joseph (1848 in Birmingham). The couple went on to have nine more children born in Nottingham: Susanna (1849), Frederick (1851), Frances Anne – known as Fanny (1853), Emma (1855), Clara Ann (1857), George Herbert – known as Herbert (1859), Thomas Arthur – known as Arthur (1862), Charles Albert (1863) and Ernest Leonard (1866).

Business flourished, and by 1871, Joseph's employees amounted to twelve men and eight women. He also had a smallware establishment at 35 Clumber Street and another branch at *'The Paris Arcade'* at 5 Long Row.

An 1868 newspaper advertisement read *'J Wilson and Son'*, and initially, the son was most likely Joseph's eldest son, William Gibbons. However, in 1873, William took over the premises at 3 Angel Row from Noddall and Company (see page 68); thus, **Button 2 – W G Wilson** – would have been one of William's. Tragically, his business was very short-lived, only three years in fact, as William died at the age of 31, on 20 July 1876, leaving effects of under £4000 *(equivalent to £507,500 in 2025)*. He left a widow and six children. A heartbreaking and all too common story in the 19th century.

William's elder brother, Henry Joseph, took over the shop called *'West End'* on Angel Row, and his would have been **Button 3 – Wilson – Angel Row.** He placed this advertisement in the Nottingham Journal on 7 March 1881:

Henry's wife was Isabella Jeffries Stimpson, whom he had married on 10 January 1871 at St Peter's, Radford. Unfortunately, it was not a long marriage, as she died at the age of 35 on 7 April 1883.

Henry continued to be listed in the trade directories at 3 Angel Row until 1889, after which he moved to Caistor, Lincolnshire. Therefore, the timeline for his button can be placed between about 1876 and 1889.

As for Joseph, the head of the family, he continued his business on Goose Gate until his death on 6 May 1893 at the age of 70. He left effects of £2300 1s 6d *(equivalent in 2025 = £344,100)*. His wife, Edna, died on 11 November 1893.

One of Joseph's other sons, Herbert, had been assisting in the shop on Goose Gate, but by the 1891 census, he had moved to Radcliffe-on-Trent with his wife, Emma.

The timeline for all three Wilson buttons ranges from about the 1860s to 1893.

> **WEST END**
> TAILORING ESTABLISHMENT
> 3, ANGEL ROW
> MARKET-PLACE, NOTTINGHAM
>
> **HENRY J. WILSON**
> PROPRIETOR
>
> NEW MATERIAL FOR SUMMER WEAR
>
> SCOTCH TWEED TROUSERS
>
> 13s. PAIR, TWO PAIRS 25s, TO MEASURE.
>
> FANCY WORSTED MORNING COAT,
> 30s TO MEASURE
>
> SCOTCH TWEED
> BUSINESS OR TOURIST SUITS,
> 50s, TO MEASURE
>
> BLUE SERGE SUITS,
> FOR HOME OR SEA-SIDE WEAR, 42s, TO MEASURE
>
> ALL WOOL GOODS AND SHRUNK.
>
> **HENRY J. WILSON**
> FASHIONABLE AND CLERICAL TAILOR,
> 3, ANGEL ROW
> MARKET PLACE, NOTTINGHAM

Money equivalents in 2025 - *13s = £88.44*
25s = £170.10   30s = £204.10
42s = £285.70   50s = £340.10

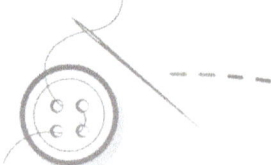

Tailors From Other Towns

ATKINSON & SON – DURHAM

JANE ATKINSON
1831 – 1905
&
THOMAS ROBSON ATKINSON
1858 – 1888

78 NORTH ROAD, DURHAM

Jane Atkinson is the first lady tailor encountered so far from the collection. She was the widow of John Atkinson (1832), who had traded as a tailor and draper at 78 North Road in Durham.

This advertisement appeared on 23 January 1885 in the *Durham County Advertiser*:

> **JANE ATKINSON & SON,**
> TAILORS AND DRAPERS
> 78, NORTH ROAD, DURHAM,
>
> IN returning thanks to their Patrons and Public generally, wish to call special attention to their Large and Well-Assorted Stock of
>
> WOOLLEN CLOTHS, TWEEDS, &c.
>
> LADIES' JACKETS MADE TO ORDER
>
> MOURNINGS and LIVERIES supplied on the Shortest Notice.

Jane was baptised on 9 April 1831 in Wolsingham, Durham, the daughter of labourer John Reed and his wife, Jane. The husband of our tailoress, Jane, came from Durham Town, and they married in 1855 in Durham. The couple had three children: Thomas Robson (1858), Elizabeth (1860 – 1868) and Fred (1872). The 1861 census records the family living at Crossgate, Durham, but by the 1871 census, they had set themselves up at North Road.

A sad story now unfolds when John died at only 43 years of age and was buried at St Margaret's Church in Durham on 7 July 1875. He left effects of under £400 *(equivalent in 2025 = £50,820)*, and Jane took over the tailoring business with their son, Thomas.

They continued to trade from North Road for the next 13 years, but tragically, Thomas died at the young age of 29 and was buried at St Margaret's Church on 19 March 1888.

Following her son's death, Jane sold the business, and the notice in the Durham County Advertiser on 11 January 1889, informs us:

> Re. JANE ATKINSON AND SON
> TAILORS, NORTH ROAD, DURHAM
>
> All Persons OWING MONEYS to the late Firm of JANE ATKINSON and SON, of the above Address, are requested to pay at once to Mrs. JANE ATKINSON, AT No. 6 CROSSGATE, Durham.
> Dated the 9th day of January, 1889.
> JOSEPH MAWSON
> Solicitor
> Exchequer Offices, Durham

Robert Smith Atkinson took over the shop; however, it is uncertain whether he was a family relation. What transpired next begs the question, was 78 North Road an ill-fated address?

Robert hanged himself on 25 November 1911 from the bannister at his home at 9 May Street, leaving a widow and family. At the inquest, it was stated that Robert had some financial difficulties but showed no outward signs of any desire to kill himself. The verdict was that he committed suicide during temporary insanity.

A tragedy indeed. He is buried in the Bishopwearmouth Cemetery, Sunderland.

As for Jane, she made it to 74 years of age, passing away on 1 November 1905, leaving effects of £2544 7s *(equivalent in 2025 = £368,500)*. Her death was reported in the Durham County Advertiser on 29 December 1905:

> Mrs Jane Atkinson, who during many years of her widowhood carried on a successful tailoring business on the North Road, Durham, has been taken after a long illness.

Her burial took place on 2 November 1905 at St Margaret's Church, Durham.

Finally, her son Fred.

In none of the later census returns is his occupation recorded; only in the 1911 census does it say that he is retired, but retired from what is unknown. He married Eliza Jane Lynn in 1892; however, Fred was widowed by 1911. In the 1939 Register, he was recorded as *'incapacitated – blind'* and living with his son William Lynn Atkinson at 1 Crossgate, Peth, which had been the family home for many years. Incredibly, Fred lived to the age of 84, passing away in 1954.

The timeline for the button would be from 1875 to 1889.

GEORGE BINNS – SHEFFIELD

GEORGE BINNS 1845 – 1912
2-12 MOORHEAD, SHEFFIELD, YORKSHIRE

George Binns certainly wanted to make a name for himself, as this advertisement suggests:

He was born in 1845 in Sheffield, Yorkshire, the son of grocer and file grinder George Binns and Sarah Brown. His baptism took place at the Cathedral Church of St Peter and St Paul, Sheffield, on 18 January 1846.

In the 1851 census, George can be found living on Hanover Street in the Broomhill District of Sheffield. He is recorded as a scholar and has an older brother, Albert Jonas (1842), a younger sister, Sarah Ann (1846), and a younger brother, Arthur James (1849). Then, in the 1861 census, George is intriguingly recorded as a pawnbroker's apprentice. However, within the next ten years, George moved from pawnbroker to outfitter and opened his shop in Moorhead, Sheffield.

Sheffield Telegraph
21 December 1880

THE
MIDLAND CLOTHING MART
(OPPOSITE THE CRIMEAN MONUMENT, MOORHEAD, SHEFFIELD.
ON ACCOUNT OF THE VERY MILD SEASON
GREAT BARGAINS
OFFERED IN
GENTS' OVERCOATS,
THE NEWEST STYLES
YOUTHS' OVERCOATS,
THE NEWEST STYLES,
BOYS' OVERCOATS,
THE NEWEST STYLES.
SPECIAL ATTENTION IS CALLED TO VERY LARGE PURCHASES JUST MADE *FOR CASH* ON ACCOUNT OF THE MILD SEASON, AND ARE GOODS THAT CAN BE RECOMMENDED BOTH FOR STYLE MAKE AND WEAR. ALSO, A GREAT VARIETY OF THE BEST GOODS OUR OWN MAKE WILL BE OFFERED MUCH UNDER THEIR VALUE.

GENT'S BLACK AND BROWN WORSTED OVERCOATS, BOUND BY HAND, FROM 20s

GENT'S ALL WOOL FANCY OVERCOATS, BEAUTIFULLY MADE AND WELL LINED, CUT EXTRA LONG FROM 15s

GENT'S SUPERIOR WORSTED AND FANCY DIAGONAL OVERCOATS, OUR OWN MAKE, FROM 25s YOUTHS' OVERCOATS (SPECIAL VALUE) FROM 10s 6d

BOYS' OVERCOATS IN A VERY GREAT VARIETY, IN ALL THE LEADING SHAPES, FROM 4s 11d. INSPECTION INVITED BY
GEORGE BINNS
MERCHANT TAILOR,

Money equivalents in 2025

20s = *£125.70*   15s = £94.30
10s 6d = *£66.01*   4s 11d = £30.93

He soon extended his premises from numbers 2 to 12, with large advertisements appearing weekly in newspapers announcing his latest clothing.

In the 1871 census, he lived at 1 Furnival Street, Sheffield, with his wife, Mary Jane, and their 15-month-old daughter, Gertrude Wardlow Binns. In 1869, George had married Mary Jane Wardlow, the daughter of a steel manufacturer, and they had five more children: Arthur George (1872), Albert Bernard Wardlow (1874), Charles William (1876), Beatrice Alice (1878) and Clement Stanley (1885). In the 1881 census, the family lived on Broomhall Road, Sheffield, a very desirable residence. George was also an upstanding member of the Methodist Church, playing the harmonium during a fundraising event in 1888 to save the Greasborough Primitive Methodist Chapel from debt.

In the 1901 census, George was at home at 7 Broomhall Road with Arthur, Charles and Beatrice, while his wife was enjoying the benefits of hydrotherapy treatment at The Hydro in Buxton, Derbyshire. The town became a very popular holiday destination in Victorian and Edwardian times, and Mary was advertising an apartment to rent at 18 Broadwalk, Buxton, in the 1912 Derbyshire Kelly's Directory. The family business appeared to include property investment, as they marketed other Sheffield residences for rent under George's name.

ROYAL VISIT

WINDOWS AND SEATS TO LET, AT GEORGE BINNS'

TAILORING AND CLOTHING ESTABLISHMENT,

2, 4, 6, 8, 10, & 12 MOORHEAD SHEFFIELD.

(Central position, opposite the Crimean Monument).

Seats, 2s 6d to 5s each

ROOMS and WINDOWS for PARTIES, from £1 1s

No Refreshments provided, access to Reserved Seats being obtainable from back of Premises within half-an-hour of the Procession passing.

Together with many other shopkeepers during the 1905 royal visit, George rented out his shop window for spectators to watch King Edward VII and Queen Alexandra visiting Sheffield on 12 July 1905 to open the new buildings of the University of Sheffield. The visit was well received by local residents, who had enthusiastically supported the establishment of the university.

Money equivalents in 2025

2s 6d = £18.10
5s = £36.21
11s = £79.66

The family, including the children, were all at home on Broomhill Road during the 1911 census, with the exception of Albert, who was married and living on his own at *'Silverleigh'*, York Road, St Anne's-on-Sea, Lancashire. Arthur and Charles had joined their father as clothiers and outfitters, but the youngest son, Clement, became a solicitor.

George died on 25 March 1912 at the age of 67, leaving effects of £218,729 10s 10d *(equivalent in 2025 = £29,210,000)*. That is quite some legacy, and a fitting obituary was printed in the Sheffield Telegraph titled:

> THE LATE MR G. BINNS - A staunch supporter of Sheffield Methodism.

It told of his lifetime connection to the Hanover Chapel, of him having been the treasurer of the Hanover Trust for over 30 years, and of how, four years before his death, he was presented with an oil painting of himself by members of the church as a token of the high regard and affectionate esteem in which they held him. Unfortunately, George had been ill for six months, and during the last two or three of them, he was confined to his bedroom.

His sons, George and Charles, continued the business after their father's death, and in 1919, who could resist '*The Bins Mac*'?

GEORGE BINNS, Ltd - Wonderful ALL-WEATHER POCKET MAC FOR MEN

THE BINS-MAC"

ABSOLUTELY WATERPROOF - FEATHERWEIGHT

35/- Can be carried in the Pocket—Folds into 8in. x 4in. Weight 24oz. Raglan Shape—Ventilated—Adjustable Strap Cuffs—Silky-lined Shoulders—Strong—Fine Texture Fabric—In Fawn and Olive—Lasts as Long—Looks as Well as a 4 Guinea Weatherproof. **35/-**

Sent Post Free for 35/- ———Money returned if not approved in 7 days.——State height——Chest measure

OBTAINABLE ONLY FROM
GEORGE BINNS, Ltd., Moorhead, Sheffield.

George's wife, Mary Jane, died in 1921 at Smedley's Hydro Hotel in Matlock, at the age of 78, leaving effects of £16,346 15s 10d *(equivalent in 2025 = £978,100)*

As for the children, **Gertrude Wardlow** remained a spinster and was only 47 years old when she died on 25 March 1917 at Bedford Street, Liverpool, leaving effects of £37,611 *(equivalent in 2025 = £2,843,000)*.

The Hydro Hotel at Matlock proved to be a popular haunting ground for the Binns family, and **Albert Bernard** also died there on 20 February 1949, aged 75. He left effects of £54,746 *(equivalent in 2025 = £2,609,000)*.

Arthur George was recorded as a retired clothier in the 1939 Register living at 42 West Heath Avenue, Golders Green, London, with his wife, Evelyn née Watson, where he died at the age of 68 on 4 November 1939, leaving effects of £62,103 *(equivalent in 2025 = £5,193,000)*.

Charles William is recorded in the 1939 Register as a retired clothing manufacturer, living at 22 Portarlington Road, Bournemouth, Sussex, and lived the last years of his life at the Egerton Hotel, Buxton. He died on 21 June 1958 at the age of 83, at Buxton Hospital. He left effects of £210,760 9s 4d *(equivalent in 2025 = £6,641,000)*.

Beatrice Alice also remained a spinster and died on 2 January 1936, also at the Hydro in Bakewell, Derbyshire, aged 58. She left effects of £37,611 *(equivalent in 2025 = £3,447,000)*.

Clement Stanley's story ended tragically when he lost his life in WWI. He died on 1 July 1916 at the age of 31, in France, serving as a 2nd Lieutenant in the Northumberland Fusiliers. His body was never identified, and he is commemorated on the Thiepval Monument, in the Somme region. He left effects of £20,352 8s 6d *(equivalent in 2025 = £1,861,000)*.

George Binns's meteoric rise from a grocer's son to today's equivalent of a multi-millionaire outfitter is exceptional, with each family member also leaving legacies of millions of pounds in today's money. Quite a journey.

The button's timeline ranges from about 1870 to 1929 and the closure of the Grantham Canal.

ARTIST IMPRESSION OF GEORGE BINNS' SHOP IN MOORHEAD
LATE 19TH CENTURY
Artist – Roger Whitehead

GEORGE BROWN – BARNSLEY

GEORGE BROWN
1820 – 1882

CHEAPSIDE & CORPORATION BUILDINGS, PONTEFRACT ROAD, BARNSLEY, YORKSHIRE

Established in 1842 – George Brown, the *'Practical Tailor'*, at 27 & 28 Cheapside, Barnsley, Yorkshire, situated next door to the Duke of York Inn. He later opened a branch in Mexborough, about ten miles away. He ran numerous large advertisements in the newspapers, as early as this one in the Barnsley Independent on 23 August 1856:

SUMMER CLOTHING!

BEFORE making your Purchases of Summer Clothing, you would do well to call and inspect the STOCK at

GEORGE BROWN'S NOTED ESTABLISHMENT

His preparation for the present Season surpasses anything hitherto offered to the public in Barnsley, comprising a Choice and very Extensive Assortment of Superfine BROAD and NARROW CLOTHS, a carefully selected Assortment of WAISTCOATINGS, comprising rich FRENCH VELVETS, Plain Figured SATINS, SILKS, PLUSHES, Embroidered VEST SHAPES, MOIRE ANTIQUES, QUILTINGS, &c, &c, in the purchase of which Excellence of Quality and not merely Lowness of Price, has been aimed at,

THE READY-MADE ESTABLISHMENT

Is as usual well stocked, and offers particular Advantages to the Purchaser – from its being larger, it offers greater variety for choice than any other in the Town. The Stock can and will be Sold Cheaper, because as G.B. sells a greater quantity, he can take less profit. He is the largest consumer of materials, the largest consumer can buy the cheapest. G.B. has a practical knowledge of the trade, which few of his competitors can lay claim to; he pays the best wages, which is the mainspring of good workmanship, and the whole is made up under his own immediate inspection.

Just received, a Choice Assortment of HATS from the Best Makers in the Kingdom. BOYS' CAPS in the endless variety. COLLARS, FRONTS, SHIRTS, NECKERCHIEFS, TIES, SCARFS, and POCKET HANDKERCHIEFS, UMBRELLAS, WATERPROOF and REVERSIBLE COATS, LEGGINGS, &c,

OBSERVE THE ADDRESS

GEORGE BROWN
TAILOR, WOOLLEN DRAPER, HATTER, WHOLESALE & RETAIL CLOTHES DEALER,

NOS. 27 AND 28
CHEAPSIDE (next Door to the DUKE OF York Inn), SHEFFIELD-ROAD, BARNSLEY

George was baptised on 30 April 1820 in Stockport, Cheshire, the son of bricklayer George Brown and his wife, Maria. Not much can be found about his early life, but he certainly made his way to Barnsley and established his clothing business in 1842.

George's wife, Elizabeth Addy Rose, was baptised on 1 February 1826 in Barnsley, the daughter of Sarah Rose. When George and Elizabeth married on 31 March 1842 in Silkstone, Barnsley, she named her father as waggoner John Addy. They had five children born in Barnsley: Frederick (1847), George (1854), Walter (1857), Alfred (1860), and an adopted daughter named Lucy, born in 1846 in Chalford, Gloucestershire.

The 1851 census records the Brown family living on Cheapside, where George is a master tailor, employing five men. The household consisted of George, Elizabeth, their son Frederick, Eliza Flemming (servant), William Rose (tailor's apprentice), Frederick Kelsall, William Carter and Benjamin Johnson (journeymen tailors). Did George like to keep a watchful eye over his employees?

By the 1861 census, the family had moved to 3 Pontefract Road, Barnsley. The shop was still situated at Cheapside, and like many shopkeepers, George fell foul of theft, as reported in the Sheffield Independent on 28 November 1863:

Still, business continued to prosper, and an advertisement in the Barnsley Chronicle on 22 January 1870 reports his removal from Cheapside to his new premises at Corporation Buildings, Pontefract Road, Mayday Green, Barnsley, which he erected at *'considerable cost'*.

> **BARNSLEY COURT HOUSE**
> FRIDAY – before T Taylor, Esq.
> NUMEROUS FELONIES – Selina Gale, of Barnsley, a rather good-looking young woman of 21 or 22 years of age, was charged with stealing various articles of wearing apparel, from different tradespeople in the town, namely, a druggist, &c from Mr George Brown, tailor and draper, Cheapside; etc… The prisoner, who was committed for trial at the Sheffield Sessions, said she had been persuaded to commit the robberies by another party, but she did not mention any names.

No. 1 Establishment contained the largest and best-assorted stock of ready-made clothing in the neighbourhood, of superior styles and workmanship, and at very low prices. Whereas, No. 2 Establishment was to be exclusively retained for the bespoke or ordered trade.

Not only was George a prosperous businessman, but he also was a member of the School Central Committee and successfully put himself forward to be elected a town councillor in 1879. However, sadness befell George when his son, Alfred, died in 1871 at only 11 years of age, followed by his wife, Elizabeth, in 1877 at the age of 53. Both are buried in Barnsley Cemetery. George joined them on 2 January 1882, at the age of 62. He left effects of £706 10s 5d *(equivalent in 2025 = £95,980)*.

His surviving sons, Frederick and Walter, continued the business as F and W Brown at Corporation Buildings and High Street, Mexborough, but that partnership was dissolved on 2 July 1888, with Frederick keeping the Corporation Buildings store and Walter remaining in Mexborough.

Both Frederick and Walter had retired by the 1901 census. Frederick died on 23 March 1914 at the age of 67, leaving effects of £6942 3s 6d *(equivalent in 2025 = £898,600)*.

Walter made it to 77 years of age. He died on 2 January 1935, leaving effects of £4973 16s 2d *(equivalent in 2025 = £465,700)*.

Thus, George Brown's button made its way from Barnsley to Nottingham sometime between 1842 and the late 19th century. What a journey!

IMAGE OF THE BROWN FAMILY GRAVESTONE AT BARNSLEY CEMETERY
Image courtesy of the Gravestone Photographic Resource Project (GPR)

COOPER – GLOSSOP
MOSES COOPER
1823 – 1906
24 HIGH STREET WEST & 28 HIGH STREET WEST & 24 HIGH STREET EAST, GLOSSOP, DERBYSHIRE

The button featured bears the name **Cooper – Glossop** and combines Moses Cooper and his sons.

Moses was born about 1823 in Hayfield, Glossop, Derbyshire. He first appeared in the 1841 census as an apprentice living with a tailor named Thomas Goodwin and his family in Charlesworth, a hamlet of Glossop. Presumably, Moses was his apprentice tailor with Thomas's own sons, who were also recorded as tailors. Each consecutive census records Moses living in Charlesworth, and his first tailor's shop was situated at 22 High Street, Glossop, opposite the Howard Arms.

Eliza Howard, born about 1824, became his wife. They married in 1844 at the Independent Chapel, Glossop, and the couple had seven children: Abel (1845), Edwin (1847), Mary (1850), John (1853), Elizabeth Sarah (1855), James William (1857), and Moses Jnr (1861).

With a large family to feed, Moses needed to keep the orders coming, and he advertised in the Glossop Record on 3 March 1860:

MOSES COOPER
TAILOR AND WOOLLEN DRAPER
CHARLESWORTH

RETURNS his grateful acknowledgements to the Public for his liberal support hitherto bestowed on him, and hopes, by strictly adhering to all orders given to him, merit a greater share of public patronage.

N.B. – M.C. is always able to supply his numerous customers with every description of Broad and Narrow CLOTHS, CORDS and MOLESKINS, which he can offer with the greatest confidence. Always having his work done under his own inspection, he can warrant it to be equal to that of any other house in the trade.

MOSES COOPER.

Charlesworth, February, 1860

Obviously an enterprising man, Moses advertised his latest business venture in the Glossop Record on 14 July 1860:

> PUBLIC NOTICE
>
> ## NEW TEA AND GROCERY WAREHOUSE
>
> THE Inhabitants of Charlesworth and the surrounding districts are respectfully informed that the Shop formerly occupied by the late WILLIAM BANCROFT will be RE-OPENED by MOSES COOPER on FRIDAY next, with a Selection of TEAS, COFFEES and GENERAL GROCERIES, which for the Price and Quality, cannot be surpassed by any other town or country. The inhabitants of Charlesworth may, therefore, save both time, labour, and expense by purchasing their groceries at this Establishment.
>
> M.C. calls particular attention to his choice mixture of TEA, at 4s. per pound *(equivalent in 2025 = £25.34)* or 1s. per quarter *(equivalent in 2025 = £6.33)*. This Tea is purchased by hundreds in Stockport (from whence this Establishment is supplied) and the surrounding districts; and it is acknowledged to be the best and most economical Tea that can be obtained.
>
> There will also be at this Establishment a constant supply of IRISH BUTTER, good in quality and low in price.
>
> Prime Old Malt PICKLING VINEGAR, at 4d. Per quart *(equivalent in 2025 = £2.15)*; and all other articles in the trade equally cheap.
>
> The patronage and support of the Public is kindly solicited.

Nicely situated, Moses's firms continued to thrive, and on 23 April 1870, he took over the property next door at number 24 High Street from Matthew Walton. An advertisement in the Glossop Record on 28 January 1871, tells us that Moses & Son were selling a suit to measure in any colour or style from 50s *(equivalent in 2025 = £314)* and trousers from 16s per pair *(equivalent in 2025 = £100.50)*. His array of stock now included 'Mourning Orders Executed With Dispatch'.

The son in question is Abel, and he was recorded as a tailor in the 1871 census, employing three men and living at 24 High Street East, Glossop. High Street ran directly through the town centre, and a further move took Moses & Sons to 28 High Street West on 15 January 1892. The sons are now most likely to be Abel, John and Moses Jnr, and the last entry for M Cooper & Sons appeared in the 1903 Derby & District Trades.

Moses died on 20 February 1906 at the age of 83, leaving effects of £314 3s *(equivalent in 2025 = £45,570)*. His wife, Eliza, had predeceased him in 1892, aged 67.

So, what became of the sons?

Abel married Maria Elizabeth Howard on 12 September 1878 at Littlemoor Chapel, Glossop. He remained in the drapery business and is recorded in the 1891 census at 22 High Street. By the 1901 census, he was still recorded as a tailor working for himself from home at 43 Primrose Lane, Glossop. He died on 11 February 1908, aged 63, in Glossop Infirmary, and left effects of £124 5s *(equivalent in 2025 = £17,500)*.

Edwin, on the other hand, did not enter the tailoring trade. In the 1871 census, he was recorded as a spice merchant and shopman, possibly running the grocery shop that his father opened. He first married Elizabeth Beard in 1872 at the Independent Chapel, Glossop, but sadly, she died in 1879 at the age of 31. Edwin and his three children lived next door to his father in the 1881 census, and Edwin's occupation was recorded as travelling salesman. His second wife was Sybilla Lewis, and they married on 1 September 1884 at St Andrew's Church, Glossop. Tragically, the 1911 census revealed that all four of their children had died. Later, Edwin became an insurance agent, and he died on 2 November 1921, leaving effects of £138 4s *(equivalent in 2025 = £8,269)*

John also continued tailoring at 24 High Street in the 1881 census; however, after this he worked at home on his own account. His wife was Jane Hannah Parkin, and they married in 1876 at the Independent Chapel, Glossop. They lived at 33 Town Lane, Charlesworth, when he died on 17 April 1911 at the age of 58, leaving effects of £175 *(equivalent in 2025 = £24,040)*.

James William is recorded as a cotton weaver in the 1871 census but changed occupation and became a wheelwright. He married Sarah Higginbottom, a Charlesworth girl, in 1884 in Lancashire, and they lived in Gorton. James died in 1915, aged 54, and no probate record can be found for him.

Moses Jnr, the youngest son, worked as a draper's assistant throughout his life and can be found in the 1881 census, working for James C Holland in Macclesfield, Cheshire. In 1891, he was living with his brother, James, in Gorton, but he appears to have brought a Lancashire lass back home. Her name was Margaret Helena Moss, and they married in 1898 at the Independent Chapel, Glossop. In the 1911 census, Moses was living at 2A Town Lane, not far from his brother John, and still recorded as a draper's salesman. Moses Jnr died on 14 October 1918 at *'Calrow'* Glossop Road, leaving effects of £492 17s 6d *(equivalent in 2025 = £32,380)*.

It is sad to note that all four of Moses's sons died in their 50s or early 60s.

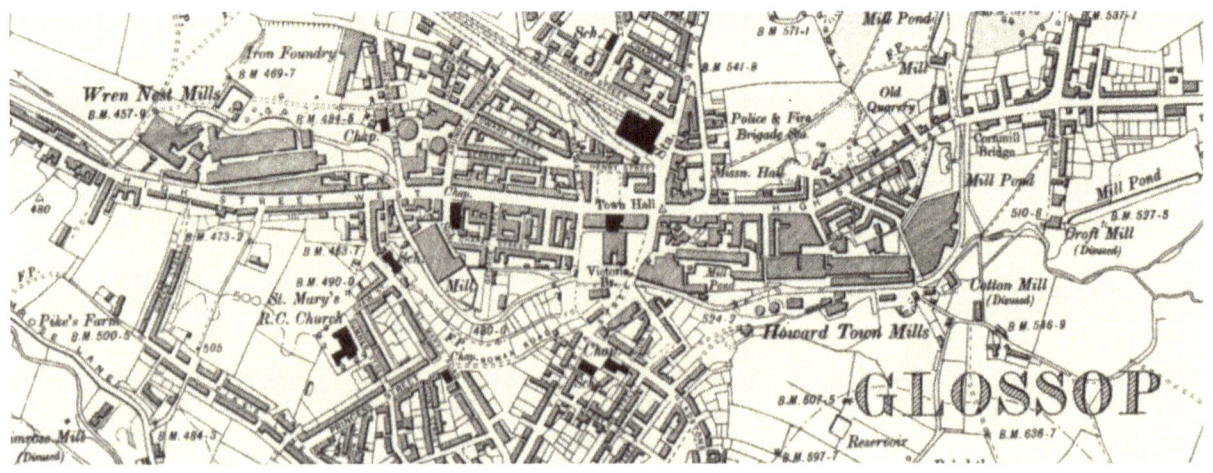

1888 MAP OF GLOSSOP TOWN CENTRE

Map reproduced with the permission of the National Library of Scotland

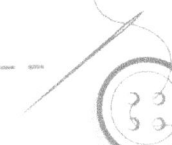

A Potted History of Glossop

One of the questions hovering around the button bearing the Cooper name was how did it travel from Glossop in Derbyshire and end up on a field just outside the village of Keyworth in Nottinghamshire?

Many of the buttons featured can be confidently assigned to the Nottinghamshire night soil, which was delivered to the fields as manure for spreading via the Grantham Canal barges during the mid-19th to early 20th centuries. Arguably, these buttons from Glossop also arrived on the field in among the night soil, which would most probably have been loaded onto a cart from Gamston.

But what do we know about Glossop?

In 1802, Derbyshire boasted 37 cotton mills, and would you believe, 35 of those were in the parish of Glossop? By 1814, as many as 21 mills were being powered by water. However, it was not until the construction of the Manchester-Sheffield-to-Lincolnshire railway in the 1840s and the opportunity to tap into the emerging and lucrative markets of China that Glossop's cotton industry began to bloom. By 1900, Glossop's weaving firms had anything from 1,250 to 3,200 looms each. A measure of Glossop's incredible industrial success was that by 1920, 80% of the working population of the town was employed by six firms, and everything seemed to be on the up and up.

Then, during 1921-1922, the Far Eastern market collapsed, the six firms ran aground, and the town that had once boasted the biggest mills in the cotton trade suddenly became the area of highest unemployment in the country. Glossop went into terminal decline amidst a global depression, and between 1932 and 1934, around 60,000 people left the Glossop area.

Somehow, this little button left Glossop and travelled to Nottingham. It most likely ended up in a privy, then onto a Grantham canal barge, onto a cart and finally laid to rest in a farmer's field until the day it was found.

The timeline for the Cooper button ranges from the 1850s to 1903.

Richard Pincott

R S Gold – Warwick
Robert Symington Gold 1846 – 1933
9 Market Place, Warwick

At The Races With Robert

Robert Symington Gold, an outfitter, JP, city council member, and co-owner of the Warwick Coffee Tavern Company Limited, was born in Warwick in 1843, the son of clothier Henry Gold and Hellen Symington. He had two sisters: Jennett McGuffie Gold (1847) and Perry Lindsey Gold (1845–1855). Their parents had married on 5 September 1842 at Leamington Priory in Warwick.

In 1861, Robert's father, Henry, employed five men and five women at his shop in Warwick Market Place. Before Robert took over the business, he had already shown great initiative during his time as his father's assistant, as seen in the Leamington Advertiser and Beck on 13 March 1862:

WARWICK BOROUGH PETTY SESSIONS
FRIDAY LAST
(Before W. Smith (Mayor), and E Dodd, Esqrs.)

STEALING A PAIR OF TROUSERS – *Patrick Ennis* was charged with stealing, on the 4th inst., one pair of trousers, value 7s 6d., *(equivalent in 2025 = £47.20)* the property of Henry Gold, tailor, Market Place. The prisoner had been remanded from Wednesday last.—Robert Symington Gold deposed that he lived with his father and assisted him in his business. About three o'clock on Tuesday afternoon, the 4 inst., he saw the prisoner standing in the corner of his father's shop. Having his suspicions aroused he watched him, and in about ten minutes saw him pull a pair of trousers off one of the rods at the corner of the shop. The prisoner rolled them under his arm, and walked off down Market Street. He (witness) followed him, brought him back to the shop and charged him with stealing the trousers, and asked him what he was going to do with them. The prisoner said he was going to wear them as they were his. He (witness) then sent for a policeman and gave him into custody. The trousers were worth 7s 6d and were the property of his father. He identified them by the private mark. He was committed to gaol for one calendar month with hard labour.

What makes this newspaper article particularly interesting is the reference to identifying the trousers by the private mark. Could the named buttons be this private mark?

Robert's father, Henry, died on 26 January 1867 at only 46 years of age, leaving effects of under £3000 *(equivalent in 2025 = £358,300)*, but his shop at 9 Market Place remained in Robert's hands for many more years.

Robert married Eliza Anne Jackson in 1871 at the Friargate Chapel, Derby, and their first child, Henry Jackson, was born in 1872, followed by Margaret May (1873), Minnie Symington (1874), Ellen Gertrude (1875), Amy Lilian (1876) and Robert Norman (1878).

Robert was an enthusiastic member of the Temperance Movement and a non-conformist. Very little promotion for the tailoring business at 9 Market Place can be found, so presumably it ran smoothly and profitably, giving Robert time to pursue his other ventures and interests. Some of these are featured in the newspapers, such as becoming a director of the Warwick Coffee Tavern Limited. *'The object contemplated in the formation of this Company is the opening in the town of Warwick of Taverns, in which no intoxicating drinks shall be sold, and which may be places for recreation and refreshment.'* (Warwick and Warwickshire Advertiser, 14 February 1880).

The establishment became known as The Dale Coffee Tavern and was a rare example of an association with the Temperance Society. Robert was the secretary, and a notice in the Warwick and Warwickshire Advertiser on 13 August 1881 informed the general public that he intended to apply for a *Billiard Licence to keep a House for Public Billiard Playing at the Coffee Tavern*. Robert was also a director of The Leamington & Warwick Tramways & Omnibus Company (Limited).

An upstanding citizen of Warwick, indeed.

Warwick Racecourse is one of the oldest in England and is held on what was once the Warwick Common, near to the castle. Robert's unbending moral belief in the perils of drinking and gambling caused quite a stir at the races, as reported in the Rugby Advertiser on 10 March 1894:

> **AMUSING SCENE AT THE RACES.** — There were some amusing incidents on the Warwick Racecourse to while away the monotony between racing on Monday. A short time ago Robert Gold, of Warwick, thought it fit to protest against racing on the Common at Warwick by removing one of the fences on the course. It is the idea of Mr Gold that there is no legal right for racing to be held on the Common, and no notice being taken of his verbal protests, he resorted to the extraordinary measure of going to the Common and, with the assistance of a few others, removing one of the steeplechase fences…

The retaliation for this incident was seen on race day in the form of an effigy, dressed in black and mounted upon a platform. In front of the effigy was a miniature fence, and the words *'Bad Gold'* were planted on a placard which was persistently exhibited. After being displayed a few times, the effigy was seized by the police and destroyed.

Robert certainly had a way about him and was described by Stephen McEntee in his history of Warwick Races concerning these protests as: *'Very much in the vanguard was Mr. Robert Symington Gold, a clothier based in Market Place, who represented what might be described as the lunatic fringe of the Temperance Movement.'*

By 1901, Robert had retired but continued to make regular appearances in the newspapers for passive resistance against various issues. Neither of his sons took over the business; indeed, Henry Jackson became an engineer and Robert Norman, a journalist.

Robert and Eliza celebrated their diamond wedding anniversary in 1931, but sadly, Robert died two years later on 9 December 1933 at the old age of 90. He left effects of £2841 15s *(equivalent in 2025 = £272,100)*. He survived his wife by only a few months. Eliza had died on 6 February 1933, aged 81, leaving effects of (£5806 4s 9d *(equivalent in 2025 = £556,000)*.

An interesting character and very much of his time.

The timeline for his button ranges from about 1867 to 1901.

'A LUNATIC FRINGE OF THE TEMPERANCE MOVEMENT'
Artist – Steve Wells

J Hawkridge – Derby
Joseph Hawkridge
1825 – 1882
24 St Mary's Gate & 8 Curzon Street, Derby

Joseph came from an old and respected Derby family. He was born on 9 January 1825 and baptised on 27 February 1825 at the Brookside Independent Chapel, Derby. His parents were Thomas, a tailor, and Betty Shenton. Joseph had several older and younger siblings, and they lived on St Mary's Gate, Derby, from where the family tailoring business was carried out.

In the 1841 census, Joseph was already recorded as a tailor's apprentice at the age of 15. In 1847, he married Sarah Ann Hall at the Brookside Chapel, and they had nine children: Sarah Anne Rhoda (1848), Thomas (1850, who died on 2 August 1861, aged 11), Joseph (1852), Fanny (1854), Charles (1856, who died in 1857, aged one), George (1858), Ada (1860), Percy (1862), and Herbert (1866, who died on 15 October 1868, aged two years and nine months).

The family first lived at 24 Mary's Gate but had moved to 8 Curzon Street by the 1871 census, in which Joseph is recorded as a tailor and draper. They continued to live on Curzon Street and seemingly lived a quiet and respectable life. Joseph died at the age of 56, on 17 November 1882, leaving effects of £238 6s 2d *(equivalent in 2025 = £32,370)*. His wife, Sarah Ann, joined him on 23 April 1908 at the age of 81, and they are both buried in the Nottingham Road Cemetery, Chaddeson, along with their son, Thomas.

Although Joseph did not live to a great age, if he had, he would certainly have been proud of his family, albeit also tinged with some sadness. Thankfully, his son, George, continued the family tailoring business on Curzon Street until his death on 21 June 1935. He left a widow, Euphemia Grace née Parkinson. The year 1935 was tragic for the family, as Joseph Jnr and his sister, Fanny Haynes, also died within a few months of each other.

The youngest son, Percy, set off on a different path that took him to Clare College, Cambridge. After his early schooling at Derby School, he commenced work as a junior clerk in the Midland Railway Company; however, his passion for science was so great that he returned to school to pursue his studies. He gained several scholarships before he went to Cambridge, where he obtained his B.A. in Natural Sciences in 1886, an M.A. in 1890 and finally, a BSc in 1889. He then took employment as a chemistry lecturer at Newcastle-on-Tyne but returned to his hometown of Derby to work as the Secretary of the Technical Education Committee for the Derbyshire County Council.

A prominent man in Derby, with a promising career, his life was tragically cut short at the age of 34, on 10 August 1897. It was reported in the newspaper that *'his death occurred following a severe illness and a most painful operation.'*

This story must surely not come to an end without mentioning Joseph's grandson, Douglas Leighton Hawkridge, George's son. From an early age, he showed great musical talent and earned a name for himself as an organist, becoming the organist and director of the Ilford Parish Church choir at the age of 21. His photograph appeared in the Derby Telegraph on 18 September 1929 with the headline, DERBY MUSICIAN TO BROADCAST. Douglas was to broadcast an organ recital from St Marylebone. His programme was to last for half an hour, playing Foccata and Fugue in D Minor (Bach), Canon in B Minor (Schumann) and Overture Athalia (Handel) – quite an achievement for a young man.

Joseph's button would have been in use from about the 1850s to 1882.

GRAVESTONE OF JOSEPH HAWKRIDGE

*Reproduced with the kind permission of Stuart Morey
Friends of Nottingham Road Cemetery, Derby.*

Headland & Co – Derby

Henry Headland 1842 – 1889

&

Robert Ratcliffe 1843 – 1912
Derwent Buildings, Market Place, Derby

The partnership of Headland & Co., comprising Henry Headland and Robert Ratcliffe, existed from about 1869 to 1881, when the partnership was dissolved. This gives an excellent time frame for the button.

Henry Headland

Henry was born in 1842 in Louth, Lincolnshire, the son of tailor James Headland and Harriett Seaman. He had an older sister, Elizabeth Marian (1840), and a younger brother, Alfred (1844). Tragedy struck the young family when James died at only 25 years of age; he was buried on 16 May 1846 at South Elkington.

With three small children to raise, Harriett moved to Worthing, Sussex, and is recorded in the 1851 census as a servant lodging with Catherine Pettett, a house proprietor. Two of her children, Henry and Elizabeth, are with her, while six-year-old Alfred has stayed behind in Louth, lodging with Hannah Taylor, a housekeeper. In the 1861 census, Alfred was back with his mother, and the family had moved to Brighton. Henry, now 19 years old, is recorded as a tailor, and his mother as a lodging housekeeper. Within the next ten years, Henry rose to become a tailor employing 16 men and three boys and was recorded in the 1871 census living on Darwin Terrace, Derby, with shop premises at Derwent Buildings, Market Place, Derby.

Henry's wife was Jael Loveridge Balston, born in 1840 in Bridport, Dorset, and they married in Brighton on 27 August 1865. They had seven children: Marian (1866), Louie Mary (1868 – 1874), Henry (1870), Margaret (1871), Harriett Frances (1873), Frank (1875), and a second Louie Mary (1879).

This advertisement appeared in the Derby Advertiser & Journal on 28 May 1869:

HEADLAND & RATCLIFFE
(Late with Mr. J. Lamb)
CIVIL & MILITARY TAILORS,
DERWENT BUILDINGS
MARKET PLACE, DERBY

On 5 January 1875, Henry and Robert were initiated into the Hartington Freemasons Lodge, Derby, and all seemed to be going well… Then a fire broke out! But all was not lost, as the Derby Mercury reported on 26 February 1879:

> **IMPORTANT NOTICE**
>
> MESSRS. HEADLAND & RATCLIFFE, Tailors of Derwent Buildings, Market Place, Derby, beg to inform their Customers that in consequence of the Fire which unfortunately took place on their Premises, they have handed over the whole of their Stock, etc., to the Insurance Company, the same having been more or less damaged by the fire and water. They will receive from the most eminent London Wholesale Houses an ENTIRE NEW STOCK in a few days, when all orders entrusted to them will have immediate attention.

Nevertheless, on 29 September 1881, proceedings for the liquidation of Headland and Ratcliffe began. What went wrong before the two men went their separate ways is unknown.

Henry moved to Mackworth, Derbyshire, and was recorded in the 1881 census with his family, working as a tailor. But a year later, Henry is reported to be liquidating his assets to pay off his debtors.

He died on 1 January 1889, at 1 Elm Villa, Grove Street, Beeston, Nottingham; he was only 46 years old. He is buried at the Nottingham Road Cemetery, Chaddesden, Derby, and no probate record can be found for him.

Jael continued to live in Derby until her own death on 12 April 1911 in Duffield. She is buried at Duffield Cemetery with her daughter, Louie Mary.

Robert Ratcliffe

Robert Ratcliffe was baptised on 5 March 1843 at St James's Church in Shardlow, Derbyshire, the son of blacksmith Robert Ratcliffe and Frances Stenson. His first connection to tailoring appeared in the 1861 census, when he was living with his brother-in-law, William Adams, a merchant tailor, the husband of his eldest sister, Mary Anne. Robert is recorded as an apprentice hatter and hosier.

Fast forward to 1867, and allow a love story to unfold. Somewhere, somehow, Robert met Martha Smith from Castle Donington, Leicestershire. Whether it is a coincidence that his mother came from the same village is unknown, but Robert and Martha made their way to Ireland to marry. The marriage took place on 12 September 1867 at the Church of Cullen, Tipperary. It did not appear to be a secret, as the marriage was announced in the Belfast Newsletter on 21 September 1867.

By the 1871 census, the newlyweds had returned to England and were residing at 17 Arboretum Street in Derby with their son, Sydney Harold Seymour, who was born in Derby in 1869. Bertha Geraldine, their daughter, was born in Quorndon in 1874. Robert was already in business with Henry at this point; however, before their partnership officially folded in 1881, Robert was already carrying on business alone, advertising himself in the Derbyshire Advertiser and Journal on 22 October 1880:

> **ROBERT RATCLIFFE**
>
> (LATE PARTNER OF HEADLAND AND RATCLIFFE),
>
> HATTER,
>
> HOSIER, GLOVER, SHIRT MAKER, &c.,
>
> STRAND BUILDINGS, DERBY
>
> NEAR THE GENERAL POST OFFICE

A year later, on 11 November 1881, it was announced in the London Gazette that Robert had gone into liquidation.

Interestingly, on 5 April 1881, both men were sworn onto the Grand Jury at the Derby County Borough Sessions at the Guildhall. Hopefully, they were still on good speaking terms with each other at this point.

Soon after Robert's business folded, he moved his family to Sutton Coldfield, Warwickshire, perhaps to make a fresh start and try his hand as a commercial traveller. By the 1911 census, he was recorded as a retired gentleman/provisions merchant, suggesting that he succeeded.

Unfortunately, his retirement years were cut short when he died in 1912 in Sutton Coldfield at the age of 69. No probate record can be found for him. His wife, Martha, lived to the age of 84, passing away on 27 November 1926, leaving effects of £1158 0s 11d *(equivalent in 2025 = £90,660)*.

The button would have been in use from the 1860s to 1881, when the partnership dissolved.

DERBY MARKET PLACE 1894
William Frederick Austin

Hill Bros Old Bond Street

3 & 4 Old Bond Street
&
35 Rue de Luxembourg, Paris

Hill Brothers was in business between the 1840s and 1920s. One of the earliest mentions of them in the newspapers can be found in the Morning Herald, London, on 28 February 1857, where their names appeared in the roles of stewards from whom tickets could be obtained for the annual dinner of the Benevolent Institution for the Relief of Aged and Infirm Journeymen Tailors, Asylum, Haverstock-hill.

Already, the Hill Brothers can be regarded as honourable and charitable men of London, added to which, an advertisement in The Volunteer Service Gazette in December 1859 informs that complete South Middlesex Rifle Volunteers uniforms may be procured at Hill & Brothers for £4 5s *(equivalent in 2025 = £574.00)*.

So, who were the Hill Brothers, and what was their story?

Henry Hill – the founder of Hill Bros

The eldest of the brothers was Henry Hill, born c. 1813 in Cullompton, Devon. His baptism took place on 15 May 1815 at St Andrew's, Cullompton, the son of harness maker Henry Hill and his wife, Mary. Henry's sister, Ann, was baptised on the same day, but she was likely the elder child. Next born were Charles, baptised on 25 January 1818, and William, baptised on 14 April 1822, both in a Presbyterian church, and their father's occupation had changed to a stationer.

Then sadness struck the youngsters when their mother, Mary, died at only 30 years of age and was buried on 26 July 1822 in Cullompton. However, Henry Snr took a second wife, Sarah Mortimer, on 22 April 1824. They married at the Holy Trinity Church, Exeter, and had two children: Edward Mortimer Hill, born 1 July 1825, and Sarah Mortimer Hill, born 15 August 1827 in Cullompton. Both had non-conformist baptisms where Henry Snr's occupation was recorded as a bookseller. The marriage only lasted eight years, as Henry Snr died in 1832 aged 41; he was buried on 30 August. Again, the record is non-conformist.

In the 1841 census, Henry Jnr is recorded living in St James, Westminster, London, and working as a tailor, but how did he arrive there?

Henry made his way to London in 1834 during the reign of William IV, having travelled by steamship from Topsham, near Exeter, with less than half a crown *(equivalent in 2025 = £16.20)* in his pocket. He struggled in his early years, not always being able to find work, but he did marry. His wife was Charlotte Barratt, born in 1814 in Sidmouth, Devon, and the marriage took place on 13 July 1840, at St Martin in the Fields, London. They were living in a time of immense change during the Industrial Revolution and the crowning of Queen Victoria, and somehow, success came Henry's way, as by the 1851 census, he was living on Charlotte Street, London, and recorded as a tailor employing 40 men, with a shop established at 3 & 4 Old Bond Street. One of his employees was his brother-in-law, Edwin Barratt. He later began his own business during the 1880s on Church Street, Sidmouth, continuing to advertise himself as *'late of Hill Brothers'*.

Before long, Henry formed a partnership with Richard Millard, and they founded a business based at 7 Duncannon Street. It is said that Millard met Henry Hill in about 1853 and that Henry suggested they form a partnership using his £1000 capital *(equivalent in 2025 = £136,500)*. Henry's younger brother, William, was to join the partnership once it had been established for three years.

Soon, large advertisements appeared, such as this one, in the Army and Navy Gazette:

> HILL and MILLARD'S PORTABLE MILITARY FURNITURE WAREHOUSES, 7, DUNCANNON-STREET, corner of Trafalgar Square, opposite St Martin's Church.
>
> HILL and MILLARDS SOLID LEATHER PORTMANTEAUS with four compartments, the Best and Cheapest
>
> HILL and MILLARDS REGISTERED ARM CHAIR 7, DUNCANNON-STREET, corner of Trafalgar Square, opposite St Martin's Church.
>
> HILL and MILLARDS REGISTERED WRITING CASE, IMPROVED DISPATCH BOXES, DRESSING CASES &c.
>
> HILL and MILLARD BEG TO INFORM officers of MILITIA that they can be furnished with every requisite for the forthcoming camp, at the PORTABLE MILITARY FURNITURE WAREHOUSES 7, DUNCANNON-STREET, corner of Trafalgar Square, opposite St Martin's Church.
>
> HILL & MILLARD beg to RETURN their grateful THANKS to the Officers of the three regiments of Foot Guards for the patronage so liberally bestowed on them during the past week.

Thus, Hill & Millard became celebrated as one of the best names in campaign military furniture, describing themselves as naval, military and general outfitters, portmanteau, travelling and dressing case manufacturers.

Henry's address in the 1861 census reflected his success – 3 Upper Mall, Hammersmith, a large property on the banks of the River Thames. Along with his wife, Charlotte, the household comprised a cook, a housemaid, a groom & coachman, his wife and their two children.

It was not all plain sailing, as an early dispute arose between Henry and Millard over the lease at Duncannon Street. They were supposed to be joint leaseholders, but only Henry's name was noted, and the landlord would not change it. Unfortunately, this dispute resurfaced in later years and broke up their partnership.

Despite this initial setback, the business was extremely prosperous, but by 1870, Richard Millard had become increasingly despairing of Henry's excesses, overdrawing on the profits and his lack of accounting for it. He added that Henry did little work for the business and his brother, William, was *'more than useless'*, and so the partnership was dissolved in 1874. After further arguments over the lease, Richard Millard offered Henry £3000 *(equivalent in 2025 = £375,700)* to dissolve their partnership, and presumably, Henry accepted.

None of this seemed to deter Henry, as his business went from strength to strength. Labels in his garments were adorned with crests for both Oxford and Cambridge universities on either side of a royal crest. They also sold military swords.

Mind you, there are always challenges in business, and in 1862, a member of staff, Frank Timewell, was charged with embezzling over £300 *(equivalent in 2025 = £37,760)*.

Then, in 1867, William King was charged with stealing a quantity of gold lace worth about 7s *(equivalent in 2025 = £41.80)*. He had been given a pair of uniform trousers to alter, but he stripped off the gold lace and went off without finishing the job.

> By Special Appointment to H.M. the Queen
>
> HILL BROTHERS
> MILITARY & NAVAL TAILORS
> 3, OLD BOND STREET
> LONDON
> And 35 Rue de Luxwmbourg, Paris

Artistic Impression of Label

Henry had moved to Brighton, Sussex, by the 1871 census, and his abode was 53 Marine Parade, overlooking the sea. Henry Poole was living at 118 Marine Parade at the same time (see page 121). Henry and Charlotte had no children but still employed a housemaid, a cook, and a footman named Rolf Ruff. The narrative now tells that Henry was semi-retired, an avid art collector, a councillor and captain of the Sussex Rifle Volunteers. He even had a bus named after him – the Brighton & Hove number 872 is called the Captain Henry Hill.

Henry remained director of Hill Brothers until his death on 1 April 1882, aged 69, leaving effects of £250,558 13s 6d *(equivalent in 2025 = £34,040,000)*.

So, who were the brothers?

From the family's seemingly humble beginnings, all of the brothers were apparently well-educated and successful. Charles had joined the family business by 1861 as a merchant/military tailor, although his former occupation had been an accountant and registrar of marriages. He died in 1877 at the age of 59, leaving a personal estate of under £140,000 *(equivalent in 2025 = £17,780,000)*.

William was the *'more than useless'* William as described by Henry's former business partner, Richard Millard, and very little can be found about him. The 1861 and 1871 censuses support the story that William joined the business at Henry's request, as he was recorded as a military tailor/outfitter, but from here on, no further trace of William can be found.

So, with a dwindling number of Hill Brothers to continue the business, it seemed to fall upon the shoulders of their half-brother, Edward Mortimer, to keep the company torch burning, and he had joined the company by 1861. He died in 1892, leaving effects of £162,634 11s 0d *(equivalent in 2025 = £23,850,00)*.

Charles's son, Henry William Hill, known as Harry, had already taken charge of the firm in the 1880s, but unfortunately, premature deaths seemed to run in the Hill family, and Harry died suddenly in 1904 of heart disease. He left effects of £145,831 7s 2d *(equivalent in 2025 = £21,190,000)*. The firm then passed to Harry's son, Osmond, but by 1939 he was no longer in the tailoring business.

So ended over 70 years of the Hill Brothers.

This quaint description of the Old Bond Street shop appeared in the Tailor and Cutter magazine on 2 September 1915:

> Just inside Old Bond-street, off Picadilly, is located the world-famous old established firm of Hill Brothers. Messrs. Hill Brothers was founded early in the last century, and the founder was generally known as "The Lion". He took great interest in sporting matters, and was a friend of Sir John Astley.
>
> The shop front consists of two large windows. The outside is quite plain and painted black, with the name in gilt letters. Iron railings stand a few feet away the whole length of the windows, with the exception of the doorways at each end. Wire blinds cover the lower part of the windows, with the name of the firm printed thereon, and the inscription, "Court, Naval and Military Tailors." The external appearance is most unpretentious and unimposing and conveys no intimation whatever of the prestige of the firm and the extent of the quality of its clientele.

However, the story would not be complete without mentioning Sarah Mortimer Hill, the half-sister of Henry, Charles, and William and the sister of Edward Mortimer Hill. The 1861 census recorded the most intriguing occupation for her – *Photographer to the Queen*. This was never repeated in any future census returns. Sarah remained a spinster and died in 1911.

The timeline for the button ranges from the 1850s to the 1920s.

HUMPHREYS & CROOK HAYMARKET

JOHN HUMPHREYS C. 1819 – ?
GEORGE HUMPHREYS ABT 1850 – 1925
ALBERT EDWIN CROOK 1863 – 1940

3 HAYMARKET, LONDON

Advertised in Field weekly magazine on 29 November 1890 - The Clarence:

So, who were Mr Humphreys and Mr Crook?

THE CLARENCE
(Rd. No. 160,964)
A NEW AND UNIQUE WINTER OVERCOAT
FOR

WALKING OR DRIVING

NEWMARKET FRONT, SAC BACK

The CLARENCE OVERCOAT combines in a high degree the qualities of smartness, with perfect ease and comfort, and of entire novelty with the quiet unobtrusiveness characteristic of the dress of an English gentleman.

The CLARENCE (made up in Box Cloth or Kersey) is well adapted for a Driving Coat, great roominess across the shoulders and back existing in union with a handsome stylish front.

HUMPHREYS & CROOK
3 HAYMARKET, LONDON

The tailoring business at 3 Haymarket was established by John Humphreys, a tailor from Montgomery, Wales, who was born in about 1819. He had two children with his wife, Mary Ann: George (c. 1850) and Mary Ann (c. 1854).

It is in the 1871 census when John is first recorded at 3 Haymarket, London, the address at which the business thrived. His son, George, joined him, and they are listed as John Humphreys & Son in the 1882 Post Office Directory of London. But by the 1891 census, John had retired and was living at 40 Dagnall Park, Croydon, with his wife and son,

George, who had presumably taken over the business. No big advertisements appeared in the newspapers for John. However, the one featured right in 1890 heralds the beginning of the partnership with Albert Edwin Crook and the formation of Humphreys & Crook, the name that appears on the button.

But this alliance was brief. By 1895, George and Albert had parted company, their partnership having been dissolved on 31 December 1895 by mutual consent. On 10 March 1896 in the London Gazette, we are informed that *'all debts due and owing to the late said firm will be received and paid by the said Albert Edwin Crook, who will continue the business under the same firm name of Humphreys and Crook.'*

What caused the split is unknown, but with Albert Crook at the helm, Humphrey & Crook went from strength to strength.

But what happened to George Humphreys?

He must have come out of the partnership in a good financial position, because in the 1901 census, he is recorded as a retired tailor living at *'Heath Cliff'*, Barnaby Road, Bournemouth. He is unmarried but has a housekeeper and a housemaid living with him. By the 1911 census, he was still at Barnaby Road and had found himself a wife. Her name was Selina Hunt, and they married in 1909 in Hampshire. It is uncertain whether the house is the same as the one George previously lived in, as he is no longer the head of the household; George and Selina are now lodgers. The head is Fanny Hicks, matron of a home for invalids, and there are two women listed as patients, a further female lodger and two servants. A curious census return, indeed.

By the 1921 census, George and Selina had settled at Highwood, Branksome Park, Lindsay Road in Poole, Dorset, and their servants consisted of a parlour maid, a housekeeper, a cook and a nurse. George died four years later on 21 May 1925 at the age of 75, leaving effects of £82,181 7s 2d *(equivalent in 2025 = £6,322,000)*. When Selina died on 29 October 1941, her effects amounted to £93,235 0s 9d *(equivalent in 2025 = £6,227,000)*.

Did Mr Crook fare as profitably?

Albert Edwin Crook

He was born on 12 September 1863 in Forest Hill, London, the son of ironmonger Frederick Crook and Emma Goodman. In the 1871 census, Albert and his numerous siblings were living at Vine Cottage, Lewisham. The 1881 census records him as a tailor, and by the 1891 census, he was an employer, married, and living at 2 Clarence Villas, Greyhound Lane, Streatham, London.

Established over 60 years

HUMPHREYS & CROOK,

Military, Naval, Diplomatic

.. and Sporting Tailors ..

3, HAYMARKET
LONDON.

(OPPOSITE THE CARLTON)

"ANDERSON'S" New REGULATION MACKINTOSH,
Approved Pattern,
Infantry, £3 13s. 6d.: Cavalry, £4 4s. 0d.

Telephone 2866 Central

In 1887, Albert married Eliza Turpin in Epsom, Surrey. Eliza was born in 1865, the daughter of plumber Thomas Turpin and Emma Reynolds. Albert and Eliza had three children: Edwin Herbert Frederick (1888), Gerald Turpin (1890) and Gladys Lily (1894).

Sadly, Eliza died on 28 December 1905 at only 41 years of age, leaving effects of £959 12s 2d *(equivalent in 2025 = £139,000)*.

Five years later, Edwin took a second wife, another Eliza, and her name was Eliza Mary Thomas.

Following his partnership separation with George Humphreys, Edwin placed an advertisement as Military, Naval, Diplomatic and Sporting Tailors in the Army & Navy Gazette on 2 February 1901, flaunting:

What are Crook's Puttee Leggings, you may well ask?

They were leather leggings worn on the lower leg for protection, mainly for the military, and Crook advertised his puttee leggings as *'Free of Patent Charges'*. The reason for this was the result of a court case in 1900, where Edwin was accused of infringing the patent taken out for puttee leggings by Messrs. Stolewasser and Co. in 1896. The judge decided that the patent had required no exercise of the inventive faculty to produce it. A strap or other band to fasten or connect an article with part of the body had been from all time in common use. To apply such a thing to hold a gaiter in position did not involve any substantial invention. Judgement was therefore entered for Messrs Humphrey and Crook with costs.

These leggings would have formed part of the uniforms for soldiers fighting in the Boer War during this period. In 1899, Albert generously offered to the Surrey Troop outfits for twenty gentlemen, consisting of a khaki serge patrol jacket, a khaki drill patrol jacket, two pairs of khaki cord breeches and two pairs of leggings.

This generosity continued during World War I when much of the country's trade was hit hard, and consequently, a relief fund was set up by the Prince of Wales to help those in need. However, many of the tailoring firms specialising in military uniforms continued to prosper, and the workmen nobly started collections to help the Prince's fund. Humphreys & Crook's employees were part of the scheme, joining such companies as Manfield, Globe Cinema Company and Fortnum & Mason, to name but a few.

Humphreys & Crook also offered the *'Braeside'* shooting, golfing or motoring coat, with or without fur, and opened an Equipment Department at 3 Suffolk Street, Pall Mall. There, they sold camping equipment for service conditions or shooting and exploration expeditions, and as an addition to their catalogue, they now offered taxidermy.

Albert must surely have been a forward-thinking man when he came up with the idea of a profit-sharing scheme in December 1920. At a meeting of his employees, Albert explained that a certain amount would be put aside for reserve each year, and the profits would be shared among the men. It was reported that if the scheme had been in operation for the past year, there would have been £1,300 *(equivalent in 2025 = £70,430)* to divide, which amount would average £43 *(equivalent in 2025 = £2,300)* for each man entitled to a full share. This sum calculates to a workforce of about 30 people. Mr Crook also added that, as a result of last year's trading, he proposed to raise the rates of pay of those who were paid by the hour.

In keeping with colonial expeditions, or even trips abroad, an advertisement appeared in the London Illustrated News in 1928 for the *'Ky-Ko'* fan from Humphreys and Crook and was surely a must-have purchase. It boasted that it needed no electricity to create a constant breeze and would run all night without attention. It was powered by kerosene.

As a tailor for a more upper-class clientele, Albert made his opinion known about the proposed new military uniform in the Daily Mail on 29 November 1932:

> TOMMY "FREE AND EASY"
> *New Uniform Comfort*
> HIKERS SHIRT — "SHERLOCK HOLMES" HAT.

Amongst other responses in The Daily Mail, Albert wrote: *'There is nothing smart about the uniform, the trousers are too long, the leggings unsightly and the open neck untidy. A hundred men could wear that hat – and no two alike.'*

Albert Edwin Crook, of Llanberis, Selbourne Road, Croydon, died on 14 March 1940 at the age of 76. He left effects of £30,963 19s 5d *(equivalent in 2025 = £2,280,000)*. However, his sons, Edwin and Gerald, having both survived WWI, continued the business of Humphreys & Crook into the late 1960s. The last entry in the British Phone Book was in 1968, and the shop had since moved from 3 Haymarket to 22 Suffolk Street, SW1.

THE KY-KO FAN
Image courtesy of Chad Baker
https://antiquefanparts.com

Humphreys & Crook were in business for nearly 80 years, but the button featured is probably dated from the 1840s to 1929, when the Grantham Canal closed… It made quite a journey.

J W Lidgett – Wainfleet
Joseph William Lidgett
1855 – 1929
Wainfleet, Lincolnshire

The first reference to Joseph as a tailor is in the 1871 census, where he was apprenticed to his older brother, James, a tailor and draper in Broughton, Lincolnshire. It is in the next census in 1881 when Joseph is positioned at 2 High Street, Wainfleet, where he was living with his wife, Ada.

Joseph was born in 1855 in Willoughton, a small village in Lincolnshire, the son of tailor and draper Elijah Lidgett and Mary Middleton, his second wife. His first wife was Mary Good, whom he married on 27 August 1832 at Willoughton; sadly, Mary died in 1833, aged 21.

Elijah and his second wife, Mary, had at least 12 children together: Elizabeth Jane (1835-1836), Ann (1836), Elizabeth Jane (1838), William (1840), James (1841), Sarah (1843), Mary Ann (1845), Harriett (1848), Joseph Middleton (1849-1849), John (1850), Angelina (1852) and Joseph William (1855), who is our tailor of interest.

Tragedy then befell the family when Elijah died in October 1858, at the age of about 50, leaving his widow with their numerous children to fend for. To support her family, she became a shopkeeper and is recorded in the 1861 census living in Willoughton with three of her children, Harriett, Angelina and Joseph.

By the 1871 census, Joseph William was learning his trade as an apprentice tailor, living with his elder brother, John, a tailor and draper in Broughton, Lincolnshire; then, at some point, Joseph made his way to work in Wainfleet. In 1881, he married an intriguing woman named Ada Lavinia Linnell from Kingston, Jamaica, and they wed in the Potterspury district of Northamptonshire. Ada had journeyed to England from Guernsey, where she had been boarding with a general merchant, George William Cochrane, and his family in the 1871 census. She was 12 years old at the time. No further information can be found about her, which is all rather mysterious.

Joseph is not listed in any of the Lincolnshire Trade Directories but is recorded living in Wainfleet in the 1881 census. He quickly moved to 258 High Street, Lincoln, yet within a year, he was declared bankrupt. An article on 3 June 1882 in the Boston Independent and Lincoln Advertiser informed that a meeting of Joseph's creditors took place at the offices of Messrs. Tweed, Stephen and Dashper, solicitors. His liabilities amounted to £427 3s 2d *(equivalent in 2025 = £58,080)* and his assets £420 12s *(equivalent in 2025 = 57,140).*

By July, Joseph's stock was for sale:

The next record that came to light for Joseph was the death of his wife, Ada, in 1883, in Monmouthshire, Wales.

Eight years later, Joseph was living in Oakham, Rutlandshire, employed as a tailor's cutter, with a second wife, Emma, and three children. He married Emma Davies (1867) in 1885 in the Westbury-on-Severn district, Gloucestershire, an area on the border of Monmouthshire.

Sales by Auction

IN LIQUIDATION.

Re JOSEPH WILLIAM LIDGETT.

MESSRS. RICHARD HALL and WALTER FITT will SELL by AUCTION, at the MASONIC HALL, on SATURDAY, JULY 15th, 1882, the remainder of the Valuable STOCK OF WOOLLENS.

Sale to commence at 2.30 p.m.

Auction & Valuation Offices, Bank-st, Lincoln.

Joseph had travelled from Lincoln to Wales, across to Gloucestershire, then to Holborn, London, where his first child was born. He eventually settled in Oakham, where his other children were born. He and Emma had six children: Harry Joseph (1886 Holborn), Lilian (1888), Elsie (1892), Effie (1892), Ernest Middleton (1898) and Frank Bertram (1900).

Bromley Villa, 60 South Street, Oakham, is where the family made their final home, and Joseph continued to work as a tailor's cutter.

BROMLEY VILLA IN 2025

His wife, Emma, died in 1914, followed by Joseph on 11 March 1929. A short piece about him appeared in the Grantham Journal on 16 March 1929:

> DEATH OF MR. J.W. LIDGETT. – A former well-known resident of Oakham, Mr Joseph William Lidgett, was found dead in bed at the house of his son, Mr Harry Lidgett, at 41, Buckley-road, Brondsebury, London, on Monday morning. Deceased who was 73 years of age, was for a very long period in the tailoring department of Messrs. Furley and Hassan, Market-place, Oakham, and left town about eight years ago to assist a daughter in a business at Burton-on-Trent. He went to London to reside with his son a few months ago on his daughter's death. He had been in failing health for a considerable time. The late Mr Lidgett had a local reputation as a vocalist, and was for many years a member of the Parish Church choir. The funeral takes place at Oakham this (Saturday) morning, the service at All Saint's Church being fixed for 11 o'clock.

They are both buried in Oakham Cemetery, and their headstone is pictured below.

And so, Joseph thankfully recovered from his bankruptcy to enjoy a family life with a steady job. His brief encounter with Wainfleet in and around 1881 is the time frame for his button.

Meyer & Mortimer

1790s to Present Day
36 Conduit Street, London & George Street, Edinburgh

Today, Meyer and Mortimer are situated in Ormond House at 3 Duke of York Street, St James, London, making *'beautiful clothes in the highest standards of Savile Row bespoke tailoring'*.

The company was founded in the 1790s by Jonathan Meyer, a tailor from Austria, who established a tailoring and military outfitting shop at 36 Conduit Street, London. Such was the firm's reputation that they dressed royalty, including the Prince Regent, who later became George IV (1820-1830). He granted Meyer a Royal Warrant for tailoring, which has continued to the present day. They also supplied uniforms for soldiers involved in the Waterloo campaign in 1815.

In the 1820s, John Meyer worked in partnership with William Quiller in Edinburgh, and an early advertisement in The Scotsman in 1825 tells us that Meyer & Quiller had warehouses in London, Dublin, and Edinburgh. This partnership was dissolved on 1 May 1830 by mutual consent.

Jonathan's sons, John Jnr and James, worked with him until their partnership was dissolved and announced on 2 February 1837 in the London Gazette. It would be James who went on to join forces with Mr Mortimer.

Meanwhile, in Edinburgh, John Mortimer had established a tailoring and military outfitting business on George Street, supplying uniforms, swords and firearms to army and navy officers. He also offered the only complete assortment of clan tartans in Scotland, along with Highland dresses.

It was during the early 1830s that James Meyer and John Mortimer joined forces as Meyer & Mortimer and advertised in the Edinburgh Evening Courant on 17 November 1832:

> **MEYER & MORTIMER**
> (late Meyer & Quiller)
> TAILORS TO HIS MAJESTY WILLIAM IV AND THE ROYAL FAMILY
>
> Beg leave to inform the Nobility, Gentry, and Public, that they have just received from their House in London an extensive and fashionable Assortment of COLOURED CLOTHS, for Dress and Morning Coats, FANCY SILKS and VELVETS, for Dress Vests, THIBET SHAWL and SILK-FACED SWANSDOWN, for Morning Ditto; and PLAIN and RIBBED CASSIMERES, for Trowsers.

Firmly established as tailors to the Royal Family and other respectable clientele, James Meyer ran the London shop at 36 Conduit Street, with John Mortimer at the Edinburgh branch on George Street. This remarkable article appeared in the London Illustrated News on 14 December 1844:

> GENERAL TOM THUMB. – The AMERICAN MAN in MINIATURE will return to London, and hold his PUBLIC LEVERS at the Gallery in Suffolk-street, Pall-mall, commencing Monday, December 23, and continuing through the Week, after which he leaves for the Continent. –Whilst in Edinburgh, the General was presented with a beautiful Highland Dress, of the Royal Stuart Tartan, manufactured by Messrs. Meyer and Mortimer, in which he will appear at each exhibition, in addition to his Citizen, Napoleon, and Court Dress. Admission (regardless of age, 1s.)
> *(equivalent in 2025 = £6.32)*

JAMES MEYER

GENERAL TOM THUMB WITH P. T. BARNUM

The story of our button emerges during the mid-19th century, when James Meyer can be found in the 1841 and 1851 censuses living and working at 36 Conduit Street. He was born in 1803 in London and married Mary Geoghegan, an Irish Catholic girl, the daughter of Thomas Geoghegan, on 11 April 1828 at St Mary's Pro-Cathedral, Dublin. They had seven children born in London: Maria (1833), Thomas (1835), Henry John (1836), Charles Michael (1838), Joseph (1839), Bernard Francis (1841), and Helena Caroline (1846). Sadly, their mother died on 19 April 1857, aged 51, and she is buried at All Souls, Kensal Green, London. Their home address at this time was 8 Norfolk Villas, Bayswater.

Just over a year later, James married for a second time to Cecilia Mary Whiteside at the Church of Assumption, London, on 8 September 1858. Interestingly, in the 1881 census, she was recorded as being deaf from birth. James and Cecilia had a son, Edward Henry (1861).

By the 1871 census, James had retired and was living at 42 Norfolk Terrace, Chelsea. His son, Henry, had taken over the business, and he was now living at 36 Conduit Street, recorded as a master tailor employing 100 men.

James's retirement ended when he died on 21 January 1875, aged 72, in his second home at 8 Sion Hill, Gloucester, leaving effects of under £6000 *(equivalent in 2025 = £762,000)*. Only a few months later, tragedy struck the Meyer family when Henry died on 1 May 1875 at the age of 39. The notice in various newspapers read:

> MEYER. 1st inst., At Tunbridge-Wells, Henry John Meyer, of 36, Conduit-street, Hanover-square, London, aged 39, leaving a wife and six young children to mourn their sad loss.

His wife was Sophia Martin, and they had married in 1863.

John Mortimer

John was born in London on 17 October 1809, the son of Thomas Jackson Mortimer and Elizabeth Mavor Elsworth. He had a brother, Frederick Mortimer (1825). In the 1851 census of Scotland, John was recorded at 103 George Street, Edinburgh, as a tailor employing 15 men. Only a year later, his partnership with Meyer was dissolved and announced on 31 December 1852 in the London Gazette, with John continuing the Edinburgh firm. He continued to trade as John Mortimer & Co., adding jewellery to his available purchases, until his death in about 1877.

Meyer & Mortimer continued at Conduit Street, but after the sudden death of Meyer's son, Henry, he had no adult son to take over the London shop.

The story can now be taken up at the time of the 1881 census, when Frederick W. Mortimer, born in 1854 in St James, London, was found living at 36 Conduit Street with his wife, Janet Knox. His occupation was recorded as a master tailor, employing 91 work people.

So, who was Frederick, and what was his connection with the Mortimers in Edinburgh and the Meyer & Mortimer business?

Frederick William Mortimer was John Mortimer's nephew, the son of Frederick Mortimer (1825) and Clara Sherwood. The 1841 census of Scotland revealed the Edinburgh connection when Frederick was recorded as an apprentice clothier, living at 35 Ann Street, Edinburgh. Residing with him were his mother, Elizabeth (1786), and a sister, Mary (1811). Importantly, they were all recorded as being born in England. Frederick Snr (1825) had moved from Edinburgh back to London by the 1851 census and was already recorded as a tailor employing seven men. The 1852 Post Office Directory of London lists Frederick under Meyer & Mortimer. Thus, the partnership between the two families had remained and now continued with Frederick William at the helm.

In the 1891 census, he and his wife, Janet, were enjoying some recreation time in Littlehampton, Sussex, staying in a lodging house and perhaps visiting Frederick Snr, who was living at the Beach House. Littlehampton was also a popular place for the healing powers of bathing. If Frederick did bathe, it unfortunately did not help his untimely death on 2 August 1900, at the age of 47. He left effects of £57,095 13s 6d *(equivalent in 2025 = £8,332,000)*

The firm continued to trade at 36 Conduit Street, and the employees even started their own football team named Meyer & Mortimer, playing in the Regent's Park Football Association.

An article in The Tailor's Cutter on 17 June 1915 describes the shop:

> ### Examples of Shop Fronts and Window Dressing
> Messrs. Meyer and Mortimer's is quite an unpretentious shop-front, evidently formerly a private residence, and now so little altered that one has to look twice to see whether it really is the abode of a firm of high-class tailors. The front is coloured in cream and brown, and, as will be observed, the royal coat of arms occupies a prominent position between the windows. Underneath are inscribed the words, "By Special Appointment", Messrs. Meyer and Mortimer were tailors to his late Majesty King Edward, and perform the same office to his Royal Highness, the Prince of Wales.

Sadly, the shop at Conduit Street was destroyed during the Blitz of World War Two, along with most of its historical archives. Further information about Meyer & Mortimer can be found on their website at *www.meyerandmortimer.com*

Like some of the other buttons, this one is hard to date, as it could have been in use from the mid-19th century through to the closure of the Grantham Canal in 1929.

AND THEY WORE THEM WELL!

Two famous gentlemen known to wear a Meyer & Mortimer suit.

CARY GRANT
HOLLYWOOD ACTOR

BEAU BRUMMELL
REGENCY DANDY

H Poole & Co
Henry Poole
1806 – Present Day
Savile Row, London

Tailors of Global Renown

Henry Poole & Co. can still be found at 15 Savile Row today (2025), declaring –

'Our clients throughout the world have experienced true bespoke tailoring, of which Henry Poole & Co. prides itself. Every item is hand-made by a master craftsman at our Savile Row premises to the client's individual pattern.'

James Poole, a young man born in Shropshire about 1781, founded the firm in 1806. He opened a draper's shop near Brunswick Square, London, and was in business at the time of the Napoleonic Wars (1803-1815). At this time there was no conscription, but the government passed acts stipulating how many private soldiers should be raised by volunteers to increase the local militia. According to legend, James joined the volunteers wearing a suit he had tailored for himself and which his wife, Mary, had stitched. It had been admired by an officer, and by the time of the Battle of Waterloo (1815), James Poole was so busy making uniforms that he set himself up as a military tailor. Much like Meyer & Mortimer (see page 117).

In 1822, James opened an emporium at 181 Regent Street, and in the 1841 Kelly's Directory of London, he is listed as a tailor and draper at 4 Old Burlington Road, his headquarters, and at 32 Savile Row.

Soldier of the 88th Regiment of Foot

James and Mary had three children whose recorded birth dates are estimated: James (1811-1813), Mary Ann (1814), and Henry George (1817). When their father, James, died in 1846, he bequeathed a yearly annuity of £130 *(equivalent in 2025 = £15,900)* to his eldest son, James, while Henry George inherited the business.

Henry began working in the business as a teenager in 1829, joining the workers in the sewing room before graduating to the cutting rooms and eventually taking down the chief fitter's instructions. He was a superb sportsman, riding in the hunts, and he even drove a mail phaeton in Hyde Park. Watching Henry mix on equal terms with the *'bon ton'* of London and dressed in Poole clothes, his father realised his son made a splendid advertisement. Henry appeared to enjoy it all, as it is on record that at a meet he found the company *'A mixed lot, a very mixed lot'*, which provoked a witty reply, *'Come, come, Pooley, we can't all be tailors.'*

After his father's death in 1846, Henry inherited the business. At this peaceful time in history, the military tailoring department moved to the back of the shop, with the front then becoming the go-to place for civilians, in particular sportsmen. In 1860, the Prince of Wales was attracted to a coat worn by an actor, thus sealing royal approval of Poole's tailoring. In 1865, Poole created the first-ever dinner jacket for the Prince, setting the standard for the DJ, or tuxedo, as the Americans named it, which is still worn today. Other notable customers were Emperor Napoleon III and Charles Dickens. They made Western clothes for the first Japanese Ambassador to London, Stanley met Livingstone in an early Poole raincoat, Winston Churchill... The list goes on.

Henry married Emma Walker in 1859 but had no children. In the 1871 census, they were living at 118 Marine Parade, Brighton. Henry's sister, Mary Ann, resided with them along with a cook, a medical nurse, two housemaids, a kitchen maid, a butler and a valet. Whether by coincidence or design, one of our other tailors, Henry Hill (see page 106), was living about an eight-minute walk away at 53 Marine Parade at the same time.

Five years later, Henry died from an apoplectic fit at his home in Brighton on 4 May 1876 at 61 years of age. He left effects of under £120,000 *(equivalent in 2025 = £15,222,000)*. However, at his death, he left £10,000 *(equivalent in 2025 = 1,188,000)* in bad debts that had to be written off.

With no heirs, the company passed to Henry's cousin, Samuel Cundey. Under his guidance, business flourished once again, and the Savile Row suit was born. A more detailed history of Henry Poole & Co. can be found on their website at *https://henrypoole.com*

The timeline of the button is broad but similar to some of the other buttons featured, and it would not have arrived amongst the Nottingham night soil after 1929.

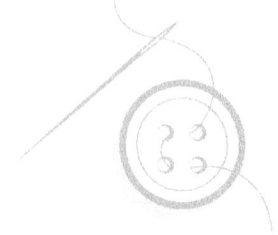

J G Rowan & Co – Greenock
James George Rowan
1824 – 1900
Greenock, Renfrewshire, Scotland

A Member of the Society of Friends

James George Rowan was born in 1824 in Borrowstouness, Linlithgowshire, West Lothian, Scotland. He initially worked as a draper and hosier in Glasgow, having learnt his trade as a draper's apprentice on High Street in Linlithgow.

He married Marion Leck on 1 February 1849 in Barony, Lanarkshire. The notice in the Glasgow Herald announced that they were married at 100 George Street by the Rev. Mr Currie.

James established a business in Glasgow at 217 Cowcaddens Street and is listed in the 1854-5 Glasgow Post Office Directory as James G. Rowan, draper, hosier and general furnisher.

In the meantime, he went into partnership with John McLachlan in Greenock, Renfrewshire, and in the 1858-9 Greenock Post Office Directory, he is listed as J G Rowan & Co. at 4 Cathcart Square. There is a John McLachlan recorded as an assistant draper in the Greenock 1861 census, while James was still living in Glasgow. However, the Rowan/McLachlan partnership was dissolved in 1867, with James authorised to *'Uplift and Discharge the Outstanding Debts'*. He continued to trade as J G Rowan & Co.

James and his growing family can be found in the 1871 census living on the seafront, at 55 Esplanade, West Greenock. The household comprised his wife, Marion, his sons Alexander (1850), James (1853), John (1855) and George (1857), and his daughters Catherine (1859) and Marion (1861). They also employed a 16-year-old domestic servant, Margaret Cameron.

As seen throughout, theft amongst the tailors was widespread, and James was no exception. From the Greenock Advertiser on 30 September 1871 in the Police Court section:

> Mary Bryce or Currie, for stealing a pair of tweed trousers from the shop of James G. Rowan, draper, seven days.

By contrast, James himself appeared before the Police Court on 11 May 1877, for contraventions of the Police Act by Merchants. James was charged with – *'hanging out hats and clothes outside the door of his shop'*.

Nevertheless, business flourished, and James's son, Alexander, joined his father in 1874, continuing as J. G. Rowan & Co. His other son, James, ran the Glasgow shop under the name of James Rowan, tailors and clothiers, but he parted ways with his father in 1878 and continued this branch on his own. He married Helen, aka Nellie Birkmyre, in 1880, and they had four children: James George Jnr (1881), Mary (1883), Minnie (1887) and Harry (1890). It is James George Jnr who will be of interest later in the story.

Meanwhile, back in Greenock, business was thriving, and this large advertisement, pictured right and taking up half a column, appeared in the Greenock Telegraph and Clyde Shipping Gazette on 4 December 1880:

The firm at Greenock undoubtedly remained a family business, with James George's other sons, Alexander, John and George, all listed in the Post Office Directory as *of J. G. Rowan & Co.*

James George had retired by the 1891 census and can be found living at Marine Place, Violet Grove, Rothesay, on the Isle of Bute. He died on 13 August 1900 at the age of 77. Interestingly, his death is documented in the Quaker Periodicals, offering an insight into his personal life and beliefs. The sum of his estate at his death was £18,660 5s 5d *(equivalent in 2025 = £2,723,000)*, and in his will, after the death of his wife, he directs his trustees to pay legacies to Greenock Hospital, £150 *(equivalent in 2025 = £21,890)*, the Deaf and Dumb Society, £100 *(equivalent in 2025 = £14,590)*, the Glasgow Asylum for the Blind, £100, the Glasgow Meeting for the Society of Friends, £150, for the distribution in Scotland of *'Barclay's Apology'* (a book written by Robert Barclay in the 17th century as a defence for the Quaker belief and practice) and other publications of the society; and lastly, the Faith Mission, £150, for mission work.

The business continued to succeed with all of the brothers in partnership together, along with James George Jnr, the son of James and Nellie. Indeed, on 10 December 1919, James George Jnr was made a burgess of the City of Glasgow and applied for Freedom of the City of London in 1929. He died in 1959, aged 78.

Somehow, this little button made its way from Scotland to Nottingham between the late 1850s and around the time of the Grantham Canal closure in 1929.

SPECIAL VALUE IN
BLACK AND COLOURED
DRESS GOODS.

J. G. ROWAN & CO.
WILL SHOW SOME
SPECIALLY CHEAP LOTS
IN
FRENCH FOULLE SERGES
AT
1s 2½d, 1s 7d, 1s 9d PER YARD
In New Shades of Grenat, Prune, Myrtle and Navy
ALL-WOOL FRENCH POPLINS
AT
1s 1d, 1s 7d, AND 1s 11d PER YARD
Worth from 2d to 4d per yard more
NEW ESTAMENE SERGES
AT
1s 5d, 1s 8d, 1s 11d PER YARD
In Myrtle, Navy and Brown, Splendid Cloth for Winter Wear.
SPECIAL LOT OF
ALL-WOOL UNTEARABLE
SERGES
At 1s 9½d PER YARD
This cloth is Indigo Dye and warranted Fast Colour, Usual Price 2s 3d
SCARBORO' SERGES
Direct from Manufacturer, in all the New Autumn Shades, at
1s 1d, 1s 6d, 1s 9d PER YARD
LOT
FRENCH CORDS AND POPLINS
AT
8½d, 10½d, 1s 1d PER YARD
HEAVY NAVY SERGES
TWO YARDS WIDE, AT 1s 10d PER YARD
BLACK SILKS
(Wear Guaranteed). Three Special Nos. at
4s 9d, 5s 4d, 6s 3d PER YARD
BLACK FRENCH
MERINOES AND CASHMERES
AT
1s 11½d, 2s 4d,, AND 2s 11d PER YARD
Several Finer Qualities at 3s 6d, 3s 9d, and 4s 6d per yard
ALL WOOL POPLINS
AT
1s 8d, 1s 11d AND 2s 3d PER YARD
ALL-WOOL
CASHMERETTE CLOTHS
1s 2d, 1s 5d, 1s 9d PER YARD
BLACK
RUSSELL AND PERSIAN CORDS
AT
7d, 9½d AND 11d PER YARD
SPECIAL LOT BELGIAN CORDS
AT 1s 5d, 1s 7½d, 1s 9d PER YARD
BLACK REVERSIBLE LUSTRES
(DOUBLE WARP)
AT 8½d, 9½d, 10½d PER YARD
BLACK SKIRTS (FRILLED & QUILTED)
AT 3s 6d, 4s 9d, 5s 11d, 7s 6d.
FELT SKIRTS
AT 2s 6d, 2s 10d, 3s 11d, 5s 6d.

J. G. ROWAN & CO.,
CATHCART SQUARE HOUSE.

Salanson – Conduit St

Frédéric Antoine Salanson
c. 1811 – 1875

55 Conduit Street, London
7 Pavilion Buildings, Brighton

The French Connection

Frédéric Antoine Salanson arrived at the Port of London from the Port of Calais, France, on 7 December 1836, and his Certificate of Arrival records his profession as a tailor and a native of France. Whether he had lived in London prior to this date is uncertain. He was born in about 1811 in France, the son of Antoine Salanson, also a tailor.

Mademoiselle Louise Feart followed him two years later, arriving at the Port of London on 2 April 1838, just in time for her marriage to Frédéric on 12 April 1838 at St George's Hanover Square, London. They then proceeded to set up a business together. Louise, a milliner, was born on 24 February 1813 in Calais, France.

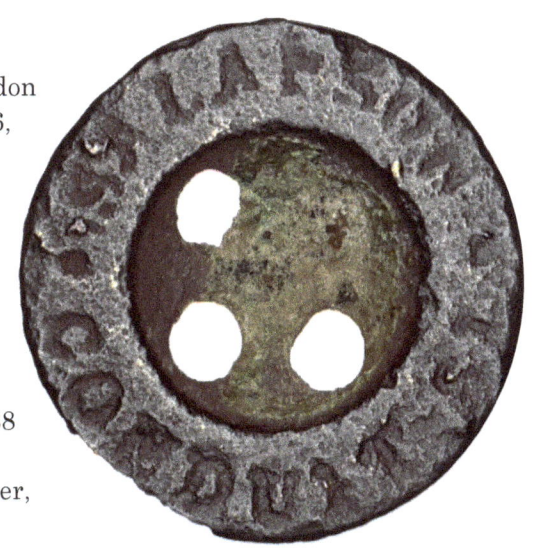

In the 1841 census, they were recorded living at St Martin Street, St Martin in the Fields, and there is an addition to the family, a daughter, Louisa (1840). They later had a son, Alphonse Frédéric, born on 30 June 1842 and baptised on 3 July 1842 at the Roman Catholic French Chapel, Portman Street, Mayfair.

The Salansons set up their home and business at 55 Conduit Street, and in the 1851 census a busy household is recorded comprising Frederick, his name now Anglicised, a tailor and habit maker, Louisa, a court milliner, the children Louisa and Alphonse, along with Louise's sister, Flore Feart, a dressmaker, Eleanore Frederick, a French milliner, Elise Capelle, a French dressmaker, Jane L'Enfant, a milliner from London, Leonide Wilmer, an apprentice, from London, Louise Marelle, a French milliner, Mary Ann Sikes, a milliner from London, and last but not least, a 44-year-old servant named Anna Flinn.

In the meantime, Frederick's partnership with another Frenchman was dissolved in 1850 and announced in the London Gazette:

> Notice is hereby given, that the Copartnership formerly subsisting between the undersigned Alexandre Edouard Le Molt and Frederic Salanson, as Manufacturers of a Patented Electric Light, at No. 55, Conduit-street, in the county of Middlesex, has been dissolved by mutual consent. – As witness our hands this 12th day of October 1850. A. E. Le Molt & Fc. Salánson

Perhaps they had invented an effective light for easier sewing?

The Salansans also opened a branch of their business at 7 Pavilion Buildings in Brighton, the fashionable place to be seen, and in the Sussex Express on 7 November 1857, this advertisement was placed:

> **MODES DE PARIS**
>
> MADAME SALANSON, of 55, Conduit-street, London, begs to inform the nobility and gentry of her return from Paris with a splendid assortment of nouveautés, coiffures, robes de bal, &c., and that she superintends for the winter season her branch established house, 7, Pavilion-buildings, Brighton.

Furthermore, while Frederick was busy sewing, Louise had developed another business opportunity with the following advertisement placed in the Morning Post on 22 August 1854:

> EDUCATION, SUPERIOR.— Madame FOURNIER, a Parisian Lady, the principal of a distinguished Establishment for Young Ladies, situate in the most delightful part of the Champs Elysées, is now in London for a few days, and will be happy, upon her return to Paris, to take CHARGE of any YOUNG LADIES whose parents may be desirous of obtaining for them the advantages of a French education. The English pupils have the privilege of receiving, independently of instruction in class, Private Lessons from Monsieur Fournier, Professor of French Literature.- Apply for terms from, and other particulars, to Madame Salanson, 55, Conduit-street, Bond-street. References given and required

As a court milliner, Louise certainly must have mixed with the upper classes of society; however, by 1870, she was winding up her business in readiness for the family's return to France. The sale of her stock amounted to £4,442 9s 5d *(equivalent in 2025 = £573,300)*

Frederick appears to have been the quiet partner at 55 Conduit Street. He died on 29 November 1875, aged about 64, at Chatou in the Department of Seine-et-Oise, France, and late of 41 Rue de la Tour d'Auvergne, Paris. Surprisingly, his effects amounted to under £300 *(equivalent in 2025 = £38,120)*.

Louise lived for a number of years after her husband and appeared in the 1881 French census, having reverted to her maiden name of Feart, living at 34 Rue de l'Aspic, Nimes. The household comprised her son, Alphonse Salanson, his wife, Adele, and their daughter, Louise. Flore Feart, Louise's sister, was also in residence.

Louise died on 20 August 1883 at the age of 70, at Saint Germain-en-Laye, Yvelines, France.

Finally, Alphonse went on to become a successful civil engineer, joining the Compagnie l'Union des Gaz in 1868, a position that he never left. Sadly, he died on 15 September 1908 at the age of 66, following a very short illness after catching a cold during a trip to England.

The Salanson button would have been lost between about 1840 and 1870.

Tautz & Sons – Oxford St
1867 – Present Day
Oxford Street, London

E.Tautz was established on Oxford Street in 1867 by Edward John Tautz as a breeches and trouser maker. The original address was 249 Oxford Street but changed to 485 when the street was renumbered in the 1880s. Edward had previously been the foreman cutter for W Hammond, a renowned sporting tailor, before opening his own shop. By 1873, Edward brought his sons into the business, and it was renamed E. Tautz & Sons. This advertisement in Field on 13 December 1873 clearly demonstrates this fact:

Edward had been declared bankrupt on 2 August 1871, but clearly the business continued, and E. Tautz & Sons went from strength to strength, despite a terrible fire destroying their building on Oxford Street in 1898. They became a hugely successful venture lasting into the 1960s, when the brand was acquired by Norton & Sons, along with Hammond & Co., J Hoare & Co. and Tod House Reynard. In 2005, Patrick Grant acquired Norton & Sons and relaunched the long-forgotten E Tautz brand in 2009. Clothing with the E. Tautz label can still be purchased online at the time of writing in 2025.

HUNTING BREECHES

E. TAUTZ (many years foreman to W. Hammond) begs to inform the Nobility and Gentry that he is still to be found at his original address

249, OXFORD – STREET.

He has NOT REMOVED, neither has he AMALGAMATED WITH ANY OTHER FIRM.

N.B. Henceforth we shall be known as

E. TAUTZ & SONS

BREECHES MAKERS, &c.
Distinct from any other in London.

So, who were the Tautz family?

Edward John Tautz

Edward was baptised on 25 January 1818 in Marylebone, London, the son of tailor and breeches maker John Leonard Tautz and Elizabeth.

In the 1851 census, Edward and his wife can be found living on Star Street, Paddington, with their first four children: Frederick George (1845), Emily (1847), Edward Henry (1848-1853), and Arthur Charles (1850-1870). Edward's wife was Elizabeth Whiley, whom he had wed in 1840 in Kensington. They had five more children: Julia Alice (1853), Edmund (1856), Charles Edward (1857-1858), William Ernest (1860) and Blanche Elizabeth (1862). Thus, the Tautz dynasty began. The sons Edward took into partnership with him were Frederick, Edmund and William Ernest.

The business thrived, and by 1879 they had even opened a shop in Paris at 84, Faubourg Street, Honore. Advertisements appeared weekly in the newspapers, with Edward always careful to state that to prevent mistakes from taking place, *'he begs to inform his customers that he has no connection whatever with any other House either in LONDON or DUBLIN.'*

Edward died on 18 December 1882, aged 64, at Mortimer House, his home in Acton. He left effects of £48,739 1s 6d *(equivalent in 2025 = £6,635,000)*.

The sons were left to carry on the business, continuing to maintain the impeccable standards of E Tautz & Sons. In 1888, the brothers were granted a patent, No. 5,068, for the *'Improvements in the manufacture of hats, caps and gloves'*. However, a few years later, not all was well, and in the London Commercial Gazette on 3 May 1893, it was announced:

> TAUTZ E & SONS, 485 Oxford-st., breeches makers and tailors. Oct. 31, as concerns W. E. Tautz. Debts by F. G. Tautz and Edmund Tautz, who continue the business.

What happened to cause William Ernest Tautz to leave the business? Well, he and his family have a heartbreaking story to tell.

Born in 1860, he was the youngest of the brothers, and he married Kate Maria Newling, the daughter of tailor John Newling, on 26 July 1883 at the Holy Trinity, Tulse Rise, Lambeth. At the time of the 1891 census, they were living in Chiswick with their four children: Ernest William (1884), Elizabeth Ellen (1887), Charles Edward (1888), and Lionel John (1895); a fifth child, Kate Edith (1886), died only a few weeks old.

When William Ernest broke away from the tailoring business, he was recorded as a wine agent in the 1901 census but had returned to breeches making on his own account by the 1911 census. He died in 1912, not knowing the tragedies that would befall his family.

His four sons were called up to serve in WWI, and as came to pass in most families during that terrible time, sons were lost. Lionel John was killed in action on 22 June 1916, and Charles Edward on 13 November 1916. Thankfully, Ernest William and Claude survived; Claude became an estate agent's clerk and died in 1958.

Ernest William's story is far from a happy one.

He had married Mary Athena Rogerson on 4 December 1915 at St Paul's, Herne Hill, and was not called up to WWI until 23 March 1918, at the age of 33. He was assigned to the Royal Engineers, Inland Waterways and Docks Companies as a clerk, but his military record did not show that he had seen active service.

A few years later, something occurred that unhinged his mind and caused him to commit suicide. It was reported in various newspapers that on 5 June 1923, he threw himself off a train near Oswestry, Shropshire. This report in the Leeds Mercury tells of the tragic occurrence:

> ## "TOO LATE! TOO LATE!"
>
> ### Man's Last Words Before Jumping from Train.
>
> The Oswestry Coroner yesterday returned a verdict of suicide in the case of Ernest William Tautz, a commercial traveller of West Norwood, London, who jumped out of an express train while it was travelling through Shropshire at sixty miles an hour.
>
> A fellow traveller said Tautz seemed peculiar in his manner. A travelling ticket-collector saw him alone in a first-class compartment and, thinking he was calling him, entered the carriage. Tautz said: "Too late! Too late!" and, opening the door, deliberately jumped out of the train backwards.

At the inquest his wife, Mary Athena, said that when he left he was in his usual good health and had no financial or other worries, and they parted on the most affectionate terms. She added that he had never threatened to kill himself and that it was impossible for him to do so. A witness on the train said that when it was nearing Gobowen station, Ernest got up from his seat and went into the corridor, going along it backwards. He was away for a couple of minutes and then returned to the compartment. He then reached for his suitcase from the rack and took something out of it. Whether it was a small phial or the end of a toothbrush, the witness could not see. Ernest took something and went back along the corridor. Soon after, he jumped from the train and killed himself.

A verdict of suicide was returned. What a tragic and sad story. Mary Athena died in 1968, aged 73, in Bournemouth, after witnessing her husband's suicide and the death of two of her sons in the war.

So, what stories did Ernest's brothers have to reveal?

Thankfully, they kept the business going. Edmund married Alice Stephens, the daughter of hotel keeper Henry Stephens, on 6 February 1877 in Acton. They did have one child, but he or she died young. In the 1901 census, Edmund and Alice were living on the Isle of Wight, but by the 1911 census, they had returned to Ealing in London. On each of these census returns, Edmund is recorded as a tailor and breeches maker and an employer.

Frederick George married Clara Priddle in 1870 in Sussex, and they had six children together: Arthur Edward (1871), Frederick James (1873), George Franklin (1874), Percival Herbert (1876), Emily Blanche (1878) and Horace Everard (1881).

A successful and blossoming family, with a large household recorded in the 1891 census living at Dibden House, Hanger Hill, Ealing. There were Frederick and Clara, the six children, a niece, a visitor, a cook, two housemaids, a parlour maid, a coachman and a groom. Not only that, but next door are the Dibden House Stables, where the gardener and his wife and daughter live. Frederick was a man doing well for himself, but not for long. He died at his home on 1 February 1894, aged 49, leaving effects of £43,201 16s 11d *(equivalent in 2025 = £6,635,000)*.

The business still continued with two of Frederick's sons, Arthur Edward and Frederick James, taking the helm with Edmund, but by August 1903, Frederick James broke away, leaving Edmund and Arthur Edward to continue the business.

Edmund died on 2 May 1915, aged 59, and the newspaper notices for creditors and anyone with debts, claims or demands against his estate revealed that he was of No. 485 Oxford Street, London, and of *'Helios'*, Castlebar Hill, Ealing, Middlesex, and of *'Bayfield'*, Totland Bay, Isle of Wight, and that he left a personal estate of £28,941 *(equivalent in 2025 = £3,128,000)*.

Arthur Edward kept the Tautz enterprise profitable and even opened a ladies' department as advertised in The Queen on 10 May 1923:

Arthur died on 14 February 1932; he had been ill for several weeks, and an article in the Middlesex County Times described him as an active Freemason, prominent golfer and all-round enthusiast in outdoor sport.

And so the empire continued with Arthur's son, Gerald Edmund Arthur, taking on the mantle of E. Tautz & Sons alongside a manager named Charles Henry Rowe. They took the helm until 1941, when on 26 November in the London Gazette, it was announced under a deed of assignment that all creditors who have not previously notified their claims against the estate of Gerald Tautz and Charles Rowe, lately trading under the style or firm of E. Tautz & Sons, are hereby required to send their particulars to Albert Whitlow, chartered accountant.

Who took over the business at this time is unknown, but it was later acquired by Norton & Sons, and the rest is history.

This button has told a remarkable story and would have found its way into the Nottingham night soil sometime between the 1870s and 1929, when the Grantham Canal closed.

J & W Todd – Bourn

John Thomas Todd 1824 – 1897
William Dales Todd 1826 – 1925
Market Place, Bourne, Lincolnshire

John and William Todd, tailors and woollen drapers, were the owners of this particular button, and their shop was situated in Market Place, Bourne, Lincolnshire, close to the Angel Inn. For a while, the spellings 'Bourn' and 'Bourne' were interchangeable, let alone 'Market Place' and 'North Street' being one and the same in various directories and census returns.

In the 1826 White's Directory of Lincolnshire, John and William Todd are listed as tailors in Bourne. William was the son of John Todd and Susannah Dales, who married on 30 October 1786 in Bourne. The couple had seven children: William (1787 – died as an infant), Ann (1789), John, baptised on 20 February 1791, Susannah (1794 – died as an infant), William, baptised on 20 March 1798, Susannah (1800) and Elizabeth (1803).

Todd's Shop Then and in 2025

Whether the John and William listed in the 1826 directory are brothers or father and son is unclear, but the early date in White's Directory rules out this being the time frame for the button. However, William (1798) is our tailor of interest as we move forward in time.

William married Jemima Campain on 28 September 1820 in Bourne, and she was a milliner and dressmaker. The couple are both listed in the 1835 Pigot's Directory of Lincolnshire at Market Place and also in the 1841 Post Office Directory. They had nine children, and all were baptised in a non-conformist church: Arabella Jemima Campain (4 May 1822), John Thomas (11 February 1824), William Dales (22 August 1826), Elizabeth Ellen (13 February 1828), Samuel Campain (15 August 1829), Mary Susanna (12 March 1831), Matilda Sophia (17 May 1836) and Sarah (1839).

In the Stamford Mercury on 8 May 1840:

> WILLIAM TODD, Woolen Draper and Tailor, Market-place, BOURN, respectfully informs his friends and the public in general that he has purchased on the very best terms a large assortment of superfine West Country and other Cloths, Kerseymeres, Doeskins, Cantoons, Velvets, Satins, Quiltings, and almost every variety of fashionable Articles for Gentlemen's Apparel, all of which he can confidently recommend both for their very moderate price and their superior quality; and he trusts that these, combined with every exertion he can make in every department to give satisfaction, will ensure him a continuance of the patronage.-London hats, Stocks, &c.
>
> The Trade liberally supplied.
>
> Mrs. TODD *(i.e. Jemima)* presents her acknowledgements to the ladies of BOURN, and its Vicinity for that kind and extensive support she has received for nearly 25 years, and begs to inform them she is now in London selecting, with her accustomed care, such an assortment of fashionable Bonnets, Ribbons, Millinery, &c. as will meet the approbation of her friends, and ensure her that encouragement it is still her desire to merit.
> Ladies' Boots and Shoes, all Town-made, very cheap.
>
> One or two apprentices to the Straw business wanted immediately.   April 30, 1840

In the 1841 census, there was quite a household recorded at Market Place. William and Jemima, seven of the children, Elizabeth Campain, who was possibly Jemima's mother, bonnet maker Ann Slayter, governess Mary Trigg, tailor's apprentice George Copping, and servants Charlotte Ward and Jane Mason.

A much smaller household was recorded at North Street in the 1851 census. William is a '*tailor and woollen draper. Firm of two employing two men*'. Jemima is a milliner employing four girls. Two daughters remain at home, Mary Susannah, now a milliner's apprentice, and Matilda Sophia, along with one servant, Eliza Pulling.

Sadly, William died in 1854 at the age of 56. No probate record can be found for him, but a notice appeared in the Stamford Mercury on 9 March 1855 informing all persons having any claim or demand upon the estate and effects of the late Mr. William Todd, tailor and woollen-draper, of Bourne in the county of Lincoln, deceased, are requested to send in the particulars thereof immediately to William's son, John Thomas.

Jemima remarried in 1858 to retired coachbuilder William White, and she died on 4 May 1881, at the age of 85, in Peckham, London.

This brings the story round to John Thomas Todd, William and Jemima's eldest son, born in 1824. He was in London in the 1841 census, working as a linen draper and listed with 12 other young men at London Street, Greenwich. While in London, he married Sarah Batibol, the daughter of Isaac Batibol, gentleman, on 4 April 1850 in Islington.

They returned to Bourne and were living on North Street in the 1851 census, where John is recorded as a master tailor and draper, presumably working with his father before he died.

Listed in the 1856 Gazetteer & Directory of Lincolnshire are the brothers, John and William, who were now working together in Bourne, and this is the only time where J & W Todd appear in the records, thus giving a time frame for the button. Their partnership did not last long, as by 1861, John Thomas had moved to Fletton, Huntingdon, and was recorded as a retired draper with his wife, Sarah, written down as a lady. Then, it becomes most intriguing. In the London Gazette on 28 June 1867, a notice appeared revealing that John Thomas Todd, of No. 5, Park-street, Fletton, Huntingdon, an accountant, was adjudged bankrupt.

In just a few years, he went from retired tailor to accountant to bankruptcy.

However, he did recover, working his way back as a travelling draper living in Peterborough before returning to tailoring later. He died in 1897 in Bourne, but no probate record can be found for him.

On the other hand, his brother, William Dales, kept the business running. He had also been working in London in his early years and is recorded in the 1851 census living with 56 other people, mostly warehousemen, at Swan Yard, Paul's Chain, St Gregory by St Paul's, in apartments for the men of Pawson & Co. to sleep in. Pawson & Co. went bankrupt in 1873. Fortunately, William had already returned to Bourne before this with his bride, Mary Ann Lunn, the daughter of William Lunn, a farmer. They married on 29 July 1854 at St Giles, Camberwell.

The shop on Market Place was their home along with their growing family: Sarah (1855), Samuel Campain (1856), William Dales Jnr (1858), John Thomas (1863), Mary Ann (1867) and Arthur Henry (1868). In each of the next censuses, William is recorded as a tailor and seemingly making a fair living. He died on 15 April 1889 at the Bourne Union Workhouse, at the age of 62, leaving effects of £530 13s *(equivalent in 2025 = £79,110)*. Perhaps an illness or disability had caused him to be admitted to the workhouse.

His son, William Dales Jnr, carried on the business in Market Place until his death in 1925.

With the tailor's shop at Market Place established in the early 1800s and continuing into the 1930s, alongside multiple Williams and Johns to research, this button posed quite a challenge. However, the names on the button are J & W Todd, and it was only during the 1850s that these two names were listed together in a directory. These facts provide a reasonably accurate timeline.

Special thanks go out to the Bourne History Facebook Group and the Bourne Civic Society for their invaluable help in finding the location of Messrs Todd's shop.

J Willson – Horncastle

Joseph Willson
1826 – 1904
35 High Street, Horncastle, Lincolnshire

Joseph began his tailoring career at Market Place, Horncastle, where, in the 1851 census, at the age of 25, he is recorded as a master tailor, lodging with postman James Gregory. Two years later, an advertisement in the Stamford Mercury on 14 October 1853 announced his removal to more convenient premises at 35 High Street, lately occupied by Mr Turner.

Joseph was baptised on 12 February 1826 at Marsh Chapel, Lincolnshire, the son of farmer Joseph Mumby Willson and Mary Sargent. They had married in Marsh Chapel on 12 March 1824.

In the 1841 census, young Joseph can be found as an apprentice tailor to his uncle, William Sargent, in Cagthorpe Waterside, Horncastle. Having learnt his trade, Joseph then set himself up in business.

His move to the High Street heralded a long and successful business venture and many years of marriage to Jane Farbon, the daughter of baker Levi Farbon. Joseph and Jane married in Horncastle on 21 March 1854 and began their family: Allan (1855), Robert (1857), Hugh (1858), William Sargent (1860), Alfred (1832), Frank Farbon (1864) and Mary Elizabeth (1866).

By the 1871 census, Joseph was employing 17 men. Like many of the other tailors studied, Joseph was a Freemason, having entered the Olive Union Lodge in 1872, holding the office of Worshipful Master. He was also elected onto the Horncastle Local Board and became a governor of the grammar school. An upstanding gentleman indeed, and all seemed well until June 1876, when an unknown altercation occurred between Joseph and another Horncastle tailor, Joseph Best. He was summoned to the Petty Sessions by Joseph Willson for an assault, but the case was withdrawn with the consent of the magistrates. All rather curious.

No apparent damage to his reputation occurred, as in the Stamford Mercury on 17 March 1882, Joseph was advertising for help:

> Tailor.— Wanted at once, a young Man (17 to 20 years of age, with some practical knowledge of Tailoring) as Trimmer, and to serve customers when required.— Apply, in own handwriting, to Joseph Willson, tailor, 35, High-street, Horncastle.

This rather splendid advertisement was placed in the Horncastle News on 2 January 1886:

Well-established and respected in Horncastle, the Willson family fared well. Unfortunately, by 1901, both Joseph and his wife became ill, and sadly, Jane died on 19 May 1902. Her death was reported in the Stamford Mercury:

Mrs Jane Willson (wife of Mr. Joseph Willson, tailor and outfitter, the Market-place, one of the oldest and most respected tradesmen) died on Monday after a long illness, aged 74.

Now, Joseph was a member of the Horncastle Guardians and had been for many years, but in the Horncastle News on 6 April 1901, it was reported that he had not attended a meeting of the board for more than six months due to illness. Joseph died on 10 January 1904, aged 77, and like his wife, he had suffered a long illness, with his extending over four years. He is buried in the Boston Road Cemetery, Horncastle, where Jane is also buried.

Joseph left effects of £6640 14s 7d *(equivalent in 2025 = £965,000)*.

As for the sons:

Robert never married and became a retail pharmacist. He was recorded in the 1921 census living and working at 116a New Kent Road, London; he had one employee, a porter. Robert died on 9 July 1933, aged 76.

Hugh also remained a bachelor and ran a book, stationery and printing shop at 25 Bull Ring. Poor Hugh came to a sudden demise on 23 November 1927, aged 69. He was found dead by his landlady, Mrs Mawer, at his lodgings at Sellwood House, which was the birthplace of Lord Tennyson. Worried he had not come down for breakfast, she entered his room and found him lying dead, partly dressed. He had apparently succumbed to heart failure while dressing.

JOSEPH WILLSON,

TAILOR AND HATTER.

Desires to call attention to his stock of

MEN'S HOSIERY

(One of the largest in the country) consisting of

MORLEY'S WELL-KNOWN MAKE, IN SILK

CASHMERE, MOHAIR, SHETLAND LAMB'S WOOL

MERINO-white and coloured — AND COTTON

UNDER SHIRTS,

Both long and half sleeves;

DRAWERS AND PANTS

In a full range of sizes, so that he can ensure a proper fit; also

KNICKERBOCKER, SHOOTING AND

BICYCLING HOSE;

LAMBS'-WOOL, WORSTED, MERINO, AND

COTTON HOSE

In various qualities;

HALF HOSE, PLAIN AND FANCY,

In very great variety,

IN SILK, WOOL, WORSTED, MERINO AND COTTON;

And, if favoured with a call, feels assured he can satisfactorily meet the requirements of any customer.

Horncastle December 5th, 1885

William Sargent had been assisting his father at the shop in Horncastle until some time after the 1891 census, after which he moved to London and married Rose Hannah Hunt in 1893, a local girl from Horncastle. They lived in Battersea, and in the 1911 census, William's occupation is recorded as a *'tailor's cutter, late an employer, now out of business'*. Rose was a sales lady and appeared several times on passenger lists to and from the USA and Canada. A mysterious 'son' was living with William in the 1921 census, yet Rose was not with him. The boy's name was Patrick Kenneth Stanley Willson, and he was born in 1917 in London, but his mother's maiden name was Hilditch, not Hunt. Then, in 1925, seven-year-old Patrick was making his way from a Dr Barnardo's home to Australia. All was not lost, as he seemed to make a good life for himself out there. He married, had children, and died in 2012 at the age of 95. The connection to William Willson remains a mystery.

William died in late September 1924, and the notice of his death appeared in the Louth Standard on 4 October:

On 2 October 1925, Rose was headed for Springfield, Massachusetts, aboard the *SS Republic* for an indefinite stay.

> **DEATH OF MR. W. S. WILLSON.**—The death occurred at a London Hospital last week of Mr William S. Willson, son of the late Mr. Joseph Willson, of Horncastle. Deceased, who was 64 years of age, carried on up to four years ago a tailor's and outfitter's business in the Market-place, He was buried at Streatham. His wife is in Canada.

Alfred became a doctor, qualifying in 1889 as a member of the Royal College of Surgeons and Licentiate of the Royal College of Physicians, and had a practice in Epsom. Tragically, his career was cut short when he died at the age of 38, in Rye, Sussex, on 28 August 1901. According to the newspaper report in the Horncastle News, he had gone to Rye for a rest and change but fell down in the street. He was picked up in an unconscious state and removed to a house adjoining, where he died from exhaustion some four hours later. His body was taken back to Horncastle, and the funeral took place on the Saturday.

The next paragraph after this dreadful news read – *Large tin Apricots 7d., Pineapple Chunks 5½d., delicious Butter 1s 2d lb – Crowson Horncastle.*

Allan, the eldest son, had a variety of jobs in different parts of England. In 1871, he was a draper's assistant in Lincoln, in 1881, a hosier's shopman in Everton, Lancashire, and a bookkeeper in a Leeds shop in 1891. His next appearance was in the Lincolnshire Echo on 8 September 1902 with this apology by his sister:

> **A POLICE COURT MIS-STATEMENT.**
> TO THE EDITOR "LINCOLNSHIRE ECHO"
>
> "Sir, Please allow me to correct the statement made at Lincoln Police Court on Friday by Allan Willson, of Church-lane, Horncastle (no occupation). He has been passing himself off as "Dr" Willson, which is entirely false. He is my brother, and we had a brother — a medical man— who died a year ago. Mr, Allan Willson for reasons of his own, adopted his late brother's title of "Dr"., but of course, under the disgraceful circumstances, it is very painful and misleading – Yours, etc,
> **MARY E. WILLSON**   Church-lane, Horncastle, Sept. 6.

Allan died aged 73, on 3 January 1929, in St Pancras, London.

The youngest son, **Frank Farbon**, had been a printer's apprentice in Tunbridge Wells. He died at only 28 years of age on 14 September 1892.

And finally, the only daughter, **Mary Elizabeth**, remained a spinster and left Horncastle. In the 1911 census, she can be found living in Harrogate, boarding at 75 Walker Road, and in the 1921 census, she was living with Sydney Plaskitt in Rye, Sussex, where she died a year later on 19 April 1922 at the age of 59.

The Willson button would have made its way onto the field between about 1851 and 1904.

Joseph Willson's shop
35 High Street, Horncastle
2025

The Willson Grave
Horncastle Cemetery

The large headstone is situated in the expensive area of the cemetery and is inscribed with the names of eight members of the Willson family.

Frank Farbon Wilson 14 September 1892 aged 28, Alfred Willson 28 August 1901 aged 39, Jane Farbon Willson 19 May 1902 aged 75, Joseph Willson 10 January 1904 aged 78,
Hugh Willson 23 November 1927 aged 69, Robert Willson 5 July 1933 aged 76,
Allan Willson 3 July 1929 aged 74,
William Sargeant Willson 19 September 1924 aged 64.

A Haberdasher

&

A Pawnbroker

R JAMES · DEALER – HOCKLEY
ROBERT JAMES 1797 – 1870
16 HOCKLEY

This is the first button in the collection attributed to a haberdasher, not a tailor, and furthermore, Robert started his working life as a needlemaker.

Robert was baptised on 24 November 1796 at St Mary's Nottingham, the son of needlemaker John James and Elizabeth. The first mention of Robert at 16 Hockley in a Nottingham trade directory is in the 1848 Lascelles & Hagar's, where he is listed as a smallware dealer, another word for a haberdasher. He would sell ribbons, tapes, buttons, etc., so it perhaps makes sense he might put his name on the buttons to advertise his business. Prior to this, he was recorded in the 1841 census living on Gedling Street, and his occupation at that time was a needlemaker. With him are his children: Elizabeth (1821), Robert Samuel (1827), Walter (1829) and William (1832), but no wife is recorded. However, in the 1851 census, Robert and the children were living at 16 Hockley, with his occupation recorded as a haberdasher. He now has a wife, Ann, born in 1806 in Sneinton.

Robert's children were baptised in the Wesleyan Methodist Church, and these records included their mother's maiden name, Ann Redhead. Robert and Ann's marriage took place on 21 December 1819 at St Mary's. This date would have made Ann only 13 years old at the time of the marriage, not impossible, but unlikely. The fact is, the Ann recorded in the 1851 census was Robert's second wife, Ann Barnes, whom he wed on 24 March 1842 at St Mary's. They had three children: John (1844), Ann (1846) and Arthur (1851), and their baptisms took place in the Anglican church. His first wife, Ann, had died in 1841 at the age of 48.

No advertisements appear in any of the newspapers or trade directories for Robert's shop, but his name did appear in the Nottingham Review on 16 July 1852 amongst the list of Burgesses, Occupiers and Freeholders who polled at the election for two burgesses to represent Nottingham in parliament. The candidates were the Right Ho. Edward Strutt, John Walter, Esq., and Charles Sturgeon, Esq.

With very few records discovered about Robert, one can only hope that he made a decent living to care for his family. He died in 1870, aged 73, and was buried at St Stephen's, Sneinton, on 15 April. No probate record can be found for him. Robert seemingly lived his life working away in his shop. What makes his story remarkable is his button – one not attributed to a tailor.

His button would have been in use from the 1850s to 1870.

T Wood – Chapel Bar
Thomas Wood
1824 – 1904
9 Chapel Bar

Another mystery lies with this button. Thomas Wood was a pawnbroker, making this a second button not attributed to a tailor. So, why would he have a button made with his name and address on it?

His shop was situated at 9 Chapel Bar, Nottingham, and he put regular advertisements in the newspapers to draw the public's attention to his business, such as this one in the Nottingham Journal on 25 March 1861:

> **ON SALE**
> **VERY FINE** and **RARE SPECIMENS** of OLD INDIA, JAPANESE, CHINESE SEVRES, DRESDEN, MAJOLICA, FRENCH &c. and other ORIENTAL CHINA, consisting of a very HANDSOME PAIR of LARGE CHINESE VASES, 24 inches high, fine in Colour and quite sound.
> GOLD & SILVER WATCHES, GOLD & SILVER GUARDS, WEDDING RINGS, SILVER PLATE, DIAMONDS, JEWELLERY, &c.
> A liberal cash price given for ORIENTAL and ANTIQUE CHINA, DIAMONDS, PEARLS, PLATE, CURIOSITIES, OLD COINS, and other ARTICLES of VERTU.
> Gentlemen having any of the above Property to dispose of, can be waited upon at their own residence, if preferred.
> **MONEY ADVANCED**
> To any amount upon all kinds of valuable Property, for Three, Six, Nine, or Twelve Months.
> Address—
> **THOMAS WOOD**
> 9, Chapel Bar, Market Place,
> NOTTINGHAM.

In fact, Thomas dabbled in everything!

He was born in about 1824 in Salford, Lancashire, the son of John Wood, a fishmonger at that time, and the business at Chapel Bar was established in 1844 by his father as John Wood & Son.

Thomas married Lucy Willey by licence at St Margaret's, Leicester, on 15 July 1845. The licence tells us that Thomas was a *Nottingham pawnbroker of the age of twenty-two years and upwards and a bachelor,* and Lucy was from the *Prebendal Jurisdiction of St Margaret in Leicester of the age of nineteen years and upwards, but under the age of twenty-one years, and a spinster.* Further details relating to Lucy told of her parentage…

On applying for the licence, Thomas made oath that Lucy Willey '*hath no Father living or Guardian of her person lawfully appointed or Mother living and unmarried or guardian appointed by the Court of Chancery and having authority to consent to her marriage.*'

It is quite remarkable what information can be learnt from various historical documents.

They had nine children: Catherine Alice (1846), Anne Elizabeth (1848), Lucy Margaret (1851), Robert John (1854), Emily Jane (1858), Fanny Ellen (1860), Maria Louisa (1863), Marian Willey (1865) and George Anthony T (1868).

Thomas's business must have been immensely successful. He put himself out there as a pawnbroker, valuer, auctioneer and silversmith, to name but a few of his specialities, and a later advertisement in the Nottingham Evening Post on 18 March 1904 read:

> **MONEY! MONEY! MONEY!**
> MONEY LENT to any amount on Antiques and Modern Gold and Silver Plate, Antiques, Curiosities, and all descriptions of Gem Jewellery, SHEFFIELD PLATE &c., AT 1½ PER CENT A MONTH, OR PURCHASED FOR IMMEDIATE CASH by
>
> **THOMAS WOOD**
>
> 8, CHAPEL BAR; and 33, CARRINGTON STREET, NOTTINGHAM
>
> Established 1844   Telephone No. 1520.

Thomas certainly amassed a substantial amount of money, as reflected in the total of his effects after his death on 10 June 1904, which amounted to £9058 5s *(equivalent in 2025 = £1,233,000)*.

But the mystery of why a pawnbroker had a button with his name on remains unsolved; nevertheless, it would have been in use from about the 1860s to 1904.

STITCHES IN TIME

Amongst the collection of buttons were several whose owners seemingly lived and worked quietly, with their stories absent from the available records used for this study. Still, their names should not be forgotten and are listed below.

John Ackroyd	1854 – 1939	3 Goldsmith Street
John Barker	1828 – 1896	113 Mansfield Road & 9 Radford Road
John Harrison Blayney	1844 – 1895	20 Market Street
Joseph Bilton Clarke	1849 – 1896	165 High Street, Lincoln
Edward Denney	1839 – 1891	Walker Street, Sneinton
Frederick Handley	1846 – 1920	6 Livingstone Street & Blue Bell Hill
James Braithwaite Hodgson	1824 – 1869	Listergate & 2 St James's Street
Henry Leake	1868 – 1942	3 Hotel Street & 111 London Road, Leicester
Thomas Nelson	1833 – 1887	20 Market Street
Samuel Neumann	1845 – 1917	7 Victoria Street
John Richard Pick	1847 – 1936	Grimsby
William Grant Ross	1855 – 1910	261 Oxford Street, West London
Henry William Tomlinson	1849 – 1922	Houndsgate & Union Road
William Vickers	1805 – 1869	7 Cleveland Street, Doncaster

Acknowledgements

I am indebted to everyone who has assisted me with this extensive project, especially the local history groups that work tirelessly to preserve the histories of their towns and villages and generously share their knowledge. I would particularly like to thank the staff at the Essex Record Office, who went out of their way to help my husband and me during our visit while we searched for Leah Groves' asylum records. My initial contact was Robert Lee (Archive Assistant), who provided me with the document references I needed and remarked, *'I must also say your method of research sounds fascinating. It is excellent to hear of your efforts to tell patients' stories in detail – certainly, they can be painful to read, but it is very important that they are accessible in the modern day.'*

This was certainly true in Leah's case.

I extend special thanks to our photographer, Steve Wells, for his dedication in photographing the numerous buttons in our collection and for a delightful day trip to Nottingham, where he took photographs of the tailor shops.

A huge thank you to the incredibly talented Field Detectives artists: Roger Whitehead, Helen Fergusson, Steve Wells, and Julie Penaluna, for their wonderful illustrations.

I would also like to thank the cemetery staff at various places for providing grave locations, especially in Horncastle, when we didn't have a plot number. A lovely and enthusiastic lady assisted us by looking up the name and location we were seeking and guided us to it.

Given the horrific events happening globally at this time, it is reassuring to know that many kind-hearted individuals are still out there, and I am grateful to all of you.

1901 Ordnance Survey map of Nottingham
With the locations of a selection of our tailors marked

Map reproduced with the permission of the National Library of Scotland

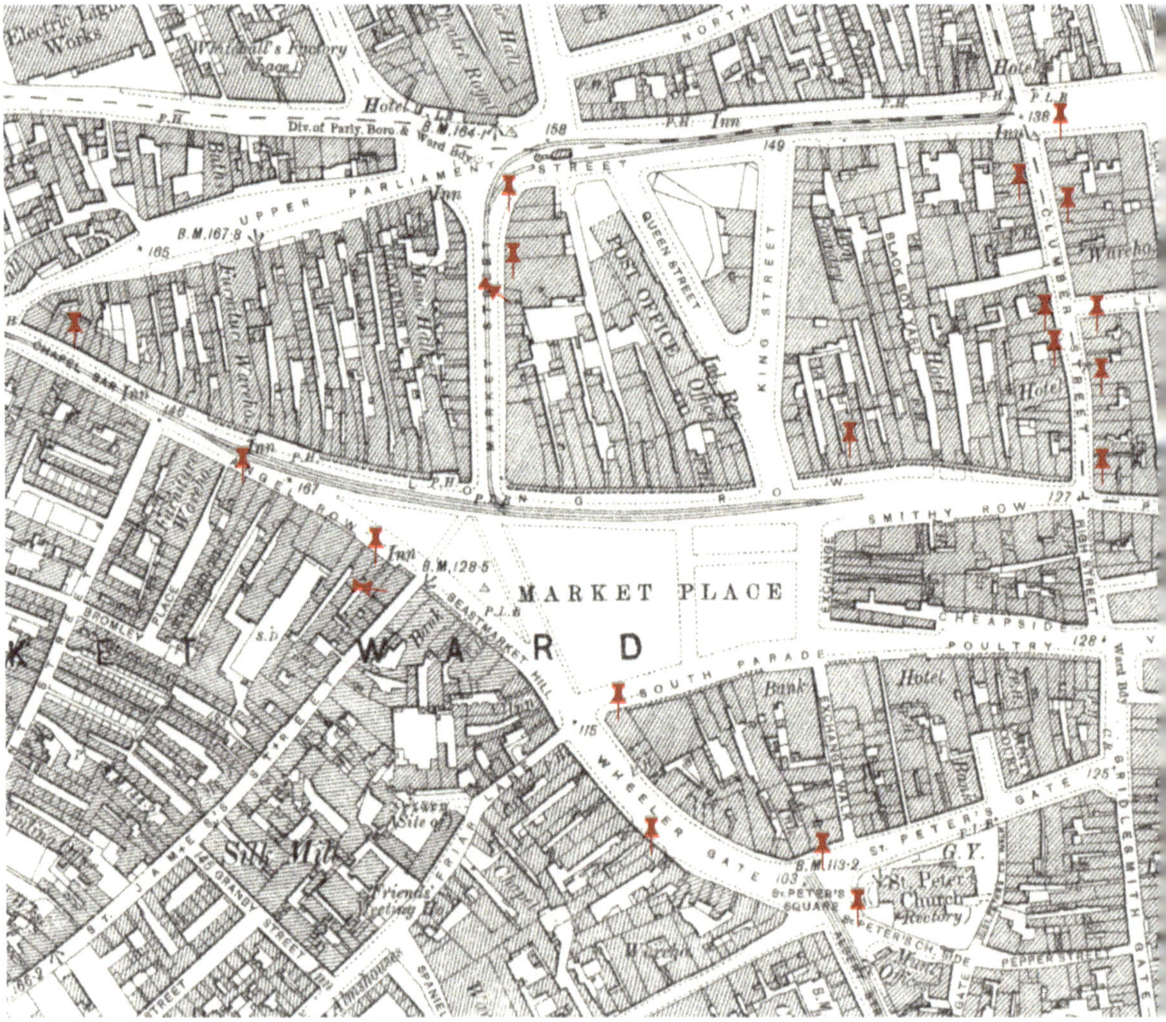

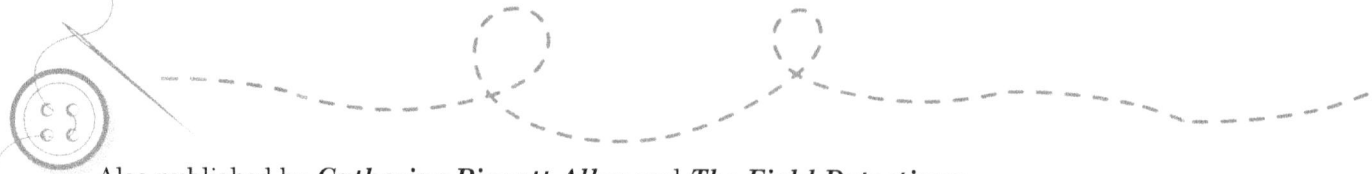

Also published by *Catherine Pincott-Allen* and *The Field Detectives:*

A FURTHER ACCOUNT OF THE HACKER FAMILY – This book is a focused research project into Colonel Francis Hacker's genealogy, primarily his direct ancestors and descendants during the 17th to early 18th century. It helps dispel some of the myths and legends surrounding their family tree. It also touches on the historical facts relating to Francis's involvement in the execution of King Charles I in 1649, which ultimately led to Francis's own execution on 19 October 1660.

THE STATHERN MOULDE CACHERS – An amusing yet informative exploration into moments captured in the 17th-century Stathern Churchwardens Accounts, which show repeated payments paid to mole catchers, often spelt moulde cacher. However, did the moles deserve the reputation they earned that led to them being caught, killed and made into various items of clothing? This booklet delves briefly into the history of mole catchers, how they went about their trade and peeks into the life of Jeffery Dallewater, one of the Stathern mole catchers.

Written by the author using the pseudonym *Emmaline Severn.*

GLORIA – An emotional, epic tale of a beautiful, passionate and headstrong woman's life story.

Set in London and opening in 1903, eighteen-year-old Gloria falls pregnant, marries the father and is thrust into the world of an upper-class doctor's wife. It would appear she has it all, but haunted by a gypsy woman's prophecy that she will never find true happiness, will her hasty marriage stand the test of time? As she navigates her family through the tumult of two World Wars and into her twilight years, her emotionally charged life is a tapestry of betrayal, tragedy, love and friendship. Through tears and laughter, Gloria's life journey from girl to woman unfolds.

RICHARD THOMAS PARKER – the last man to be publicly hanged in Nottingham

The author is a family descendant, and this is an account of the events leading up to the hanging of Richard Thomas Parker on 10th August 1864 in Nottingham for the murder of his mother at Fiskerton, Nottinghamshire. Parker was 29 years old.

STEADY AS SHE GOES – The poignant wartime memories of a WWII Navy 'medic'.

Eighteen-year-old Ted joined the Royal Navy in 1943 as a medic; he wanted to preserve life. WWII had been raging for four years, but for Ted, it was a journey into the unknown, with the threat of death a constant companion. Yet, he did not dwell on the dark side of life, enjoying himself as much as he could before the D-Day landings of 1944 and the liberation of Europe began. Told as a touching conversation between father and daughter in his latter years, this short story recounts his memories of that time.

COMING SOON – **LOOKING INSIDE WITCH BOTTLES** – a tantalising glimpse into the scientific study of the contents of witch bottles and the stories behind them.

www.ingramcontent.com/pod-product-compliance
Lightning Source LLC
Chambersburg PA
CBHW061112070526
44583CB00027B/3262